Brand^{YOU}

Human Intelligence in the Age of AI.

Forget the Persona. Build the Frequency.
Atomic-Level Branding is *the* imperative
for the new era.

Jo Starling

Copyright ©2026 Jo Starling

All rights reserved. No part of this book may be reproduced or used in any manner without written permission of the copyright owner except for the use of quotations in a book review.

ISBN 978-0-6483009-1-5 (Paperback)

ISBN 978-0-6483009-2-2 (eBook)

For Charlotte.

BRAND LEXICON

Before we begin, let's establish a shared language for the journey ahead. These terms form the foundation of atomic-level branding — the work of aligning with the frequency you were born with.

Atomic-Level Branding (ALB)

Personal branding that begins at your core — your values, traits, and inherent frequency — rather than surface-level tactics. It's the smallest, most fundamental unit of your brand identity.

Frequency

The unique energetic signature you emit — your natural way of being in the world. Like a radio signal, your frequency is what others tune into when they encounter you. It's composed of your traits, values, voice, and energy, all resonating at a particular wavelength.

Resonance

The alignment between your internal frequency and your external expression. When you're in resonance, what people experience matches who you truly are. Strong resonance creates trust; weak resonance creates confusion.

Tuning
The practice of adjusting your expression to align with your authentic frequency. Not changing who you are, but removing interference and amplifying what's true.

Signal
What you broadcast to the world — intentionally and unintentionally. Your signal includes your words, actions, appearance, tone, and energy. Strong signals are clear and consistent; weak signals are muddy and contradictory.

Static
Interference between your authentic frequency and what you're projecting. Static occurs when you're performing, masking, or acting out of alignment. It creates confusion and erodes trust.

Congruence
The state of alignment where your internal values, external behaviour, and brand expression all match. Congruence eliminates cognitive dissonance in your audience.

Incongruence
Misalignment between who you are and what you project. Even small incongruences — a forced laugh, an insincere comment, behaviour that contradicts your values — create dissonance that others instinctively sense.

Brand Promise
The unspoken agreement you make with your audience about what they can expect from you. It's built through consistent patterns of behaviour and reinforced (or broken) with every interaction.

Polarity
The natural push-pull of an authentic brand. Your frequency attracts those who resonate with it and repels those who don't. This isn't a flaw — it's a feature. Strong brands aren't for everyone.

Amplitude

The strength or intensity with which you express certain traits. You can turn up the amplitude on humour, turn down the amplitude on seriousness, or find the right balance for your intended impact.

Harmonics

The subtle undertones of your frequency — secondary traits that add complexity and depth to your brand. Just as musical notes have harmonics, your primary traits create ripple effects that contribute to your overall resonance.

The Truman Show

The modern reality where our lives are increasingly visible, recorded, and shared. In this context, personal and private have blurred, making brand congruence essential for survival and success. (For those who haven't seen the flick, it's about a bloke unknowingly starring in a reality TV show his whole life, every interaction staged, every event designed to keep him performing for an audience he doesn't even know exists.)

Aligned AF

The state of being fully aligned with your authentic frequency — living, breathing, and expressing your brand without effort or performance. When you're Aligned AF, your brand isn't something you do; it's who you are.

Also AlignedAF™ is an app you can access to take your ALB journey even further. A companion and community with even more reflections, guides and tools to help keep you on track.

BOOK YOUR DISCOVERY CALL

INTRODUCTION

Content Warning: This introduction contains references to online harassment, cancel culture, and trauma that some readers may find triggering. If you've experienced similar situations, please proceed with self-care.

The moment everything shattered wasn't dramatic. It was quiet. I was sitting at my desk, watching my phone light up with notifications — each one another strike, another accusation, another carefully crafted lie spreading across the fishing industry like wildfire. My hands were shaking. My chest felt tight. And somewhere in the background, my brilliant, funny, world-famous husband was making coffee, completely unaware that our world was about to implode.

This is the story of how I lost myself. And how, in the wreckage, I discovered something that would fundamentally change the way I understood personal branding, business identity, and the dangerous game we play when we perform instead of simply *being*.

This is the origin story of Atomic Level Branding.

When Your Star Rises, Someone Always Wants to Shoot It Down.

Let me take you back to 2009. I met Steve — think Crocodile Dundee with a few extra pounds and the mind of a professor — while doing what I loved most: fishing. At the time, I was running a successful bespoke advertising agency. I was a creative strategist, a coach, an entrepreneur. I wore my "personal brand" like a suit of armour, meticulously crafted, performatively perfect.

I thought I was strong. I was actually brittle.

Soon after Steve strode into my life with his wit, generosity, and utterly magnetic presence, I made a choice that seemed simple at the time: I folded my agency and moved south to his home waters. We built a life together. My star began to rise in the recreational fishing world. We were dynamic, visible, and — crucially — happy.

And that's when she noticed.

One woman. Someone I'd worked with early on. Someone who, after a business disagreement following my appearance as a presenter at her event, decided that disagreement wasn't enough. She wanted annihilation.

THE ANATOMY OF A CANCELLATION

What followed was textbook cancel culture before we even had that term.

She curated a posse — people willing to listen to fabricated stories about our "various evils." She weaponised their networks. Then, like a coordinated military strike, defamatory articles and vicious allegations appeared everywhere simultaneously. Social media. Industry publications. Whispered conversations at events.

The strategy was brilliant in its cruelty: make it look like *everyone* knew these things, and anyone who wasn't against us was simply ignorant or complicit.

As someone relatively new to the fishing industry, I was shaken to my core.

The panic attacks came first. Then the deep, suffocating anxiety. I withdrew from social media, stopped commenting, stopped showing up. I watched the attacks pile up and recorded them in silence, sinking deeper into a vortex of horror with each passing day.

THE TRAP: WHEN ETHICS BECOME WEAPONISED

Here's what made it truly diabolical: she was unwell. Both mentally and physically. Her pattern was consistent — launch a vicious attack, then have a medical relapse. Any response from us would look like we were attacking a vulnerable, disabled person.

Our personal ethics wouldn't allow it. So we stayed silent.

Friends and colleagues reached out privately. "Everyone knows she's unstable," they assured us. "Most people see right through this." But here's what I felt: *shame*. Deep, consuming shame. I was terrified that readers were believing these lies. That without my response, I was complicit in my own destruction.

My knowledge of social media told me that engaging would be counterproductive. That feeding the troll would only make it worse. But my fragile sense of self told me something else entirely: that my silence proved my guilt.

I felt trapped. And I've been through some horrific stuff in my life, but I'd never felt *that* trapped.

Steve and I made a choice: ride it out. Hang tough. Trust our personal brands to see us through.

We took a massive hit. But we survived.

YEARS IN THE WILDERNESS

What I didn't know then was that "survival" would cost me years.

Years of silence. Years of self-doubt. Years of staying small, playing safe, and wondering if I'd ever find my voice again.

In that wilderness, I did what any strategic thinker does when the world stops making sense: I observed. I reflected. I asked the hard questions:

Why did this rock me so profoundly in the first place?

How did I get sucked into the gaslighting?

Why did Imposter Syndrome get the upper hand when I knew — intellectually — that these accusations were lies?

The answers led me to a realisation that would become the foundation of this entire book:

I was juggling personas. And when the attack came, none of them had the ballast to weather the storm.

THE WOMAN IN THE ARMOUR

Let me tell you who I really was during that time, beneath all the polish:

I was a successful creative strategist and entrepreneur with a plethora of business awards and creative accolades. I wore my "personal brand" like medieval armour — strong, impenetrable, *performative*. I thought it made me powerful. It actually made me fragile.

When I met Steve and folded my agency to start a new life in his world, I added another persona to my collection: "Steve's Partner in the Fishing Industry." I performed that role, too. Carefully. Strategically.

What I didn't realise was that the armour guarded undiagnosed PTSD from violent sexual assaults in my twenties. I looked strong from the outside. But I was brittle. And when the pressure came, I shattered.

What I didn't understand was this: **you can't build an empire on performed identities. You can only build fragility disguised as success.**

I'll never forget the advice my father gave me early in my relationship with Steve. We were talking about my career transition, and he said, simply: *"You'll never be Steve, Jo."*

At the time, I brushed it off. "I don't want to be Steve, Dad. I want to be me."

But many years later, sitting in the rubble of my collapsed personas, I realised what he was really trying to tell me:

We are what we are.

And the problem wasn't that I was trying to be Steve. The problem was that I wasn't even being *me*. I was performing a collection of Frankenstein identities, bolted together from borrowed strategies, inherited aesthetics, and external expectations.

When the troll came for me, she didn't just attack my reputation. She attacked the scaffolding holding up my entire sense of self.

And because that scaffolding was built on performance rather than truth, it collapsed.

WHAT I KNOW NOW (THAT I WISH I'D KNOWN THEN)

Here's the hard truth: if I could go back, I wouldn't handle that woman any differently. She was unwell. Engaging would have been destructive for everyone involved. Silence was the ethical choice.

But here's what I *would* change:

I wouldn't have retreated.

If I'd been operating from my authentic core — from what I now call my Atomic Level — that gaslighting wouldn't have landed. I wouldn't have questioned my resonance. I would have had the internal ballast to weather the storm without fracturing.

The attack might have happened exactly the same way. But *I* would have remained whole. How do I know? Because I've lived this version!

Recently, one of the cronies came for us both again. This time, I confronted it, not online, in person. We've had incredible rows! But a recent interaction at a national event showed my strength. Face to face, my brand held. In fact, she asked me how I manage to "keep my tribe in line"! I told her I don't have to. We are all aligned. We stand together and thrive. Our frequencies are in harmony. There is no wrangling to be done.

And that's the point of this entire book.

THE PHILOSOPHY BORN FROM PAIN

Atomic Level Branding isn't a marketing tactic. It's not a framework for crafting a clever persona or "finding your niche." It's not about building a brand like you'd build a house.

It's about uncovering the truth of who you are at your core — your inherent traits, your unspoken promises, your resonant frequency — and letting your businesses, your ventures, your public presence, your tribe *emerge* from that foundation.

It's about becoming so profoundly grounded in your authentic self that when the storms come (and they will come), you don't shatter. You bend. You hold. You *resonate*.

This book is for the founders and thought leaders who are exhausted from performing. Who are juggling personas across platforms and wondering why success feels so hollow. Who are one bad review, one troll attack, one public criticism away from complete collapse.

This book is for anyone who's ever felt like an imposter in their own life.

And this book is my promise to you: **if I can save you from the material and psychological damage of retreating into silence, shame, and self-doubt, I will.**

Because you are not your brand. You are the *source* from which all your brands flow.

And when you understand that — when you anchor yourself at the atomic level — you become unshakeable.

This isn't a book you read once and put on a shelf. It's a companion for excavation. For discovery. For alignment.

A FINAL WORD BEFORE WE BEGIN

I won't lie to you: this work isn't easy. Excavating your authentic self means confronting the parts of you that you've hidden, performed around, or denied entirely. It means facing the gap between who you've been pretending to be and who you actually are.

But here's what I promise: on the other side of that excavation is freedom.

Freedom from the exhausting cycle of performance. Freedom from imposter syndrome. Freedom from the fear that one bad day, one troll, one cancellation attempt will destroy everything you've built.

Because when you build from your atomic core, you don't build fragility.

You build resonance. You build magnetism. You build *truth*.

And truth doesn't shatter.

Let's begin.

What This Book Is About

This isn't a book about building a brand. It's a book about *tuning* to the one you already have.

You were born with a frequency — a unique energetic signature that's been with you since day one. It's made up of your personality traits, your values, your quirks, your voice, your humour, your way of seeing the world. That frequency is your brand. Not the logo you design, not the tagline you craft, not the persona you curate for Instagram. *You.*

But somewhere along the way, most of us learn to muffle that signal. We absorb expectations from family, school, society, and culture. We smooth down the edges that make us different. We learn to perform rather than resonate. We broadcast what we think people want to hear instead of tuning into what's true.

And then we wonder why our brand feels exhausting. Why it doesn't attract the right people. Why it feels like we're constantly wearing a mask.

Atomic-level branding is the practice of stripping away that interference and tuning back into your authentic frequency. It's about recognising the signal you were born to transmit and amplifying it with clarity, consistency, and congruence. It's about aligning what you project with who you are, so your brand becomes effortless to live and impossible to fake.

In this book, you'll learn:
- The history of branding — from cattle marks to personal brands — and why your behaviour *is* your brand in the age of social media
- How to identify the frequency you were born with (and the static you've absorbed along the way)
- Why brutal honesty is essential for tuning your brand at the atomic level — and why this work is private and safe
- How to live in the Truman Show era without losing your authenticity
- The difference between congruence and conflation when it comes to personal and business brands
- How to tune your traits, adjust your amplitude, and create resonance that attracts your tribe

This is not a book about becoming someone else. It's a book about coming home to yourself.

How to Use This Book

This book is divided into three parts:
PART ONE: FOUNDATIONS
>Understanding brand, recognising the frequency you already emit, and beginning to identify the traits that make you *you*.

PART TWO: TUNING YOUR FREQUENCY
>Refining your signal, removing static, aligning your resonance, and navigating the Truman Show reality with integrity.

PART THREE: LIVING ALIGNED
>Expressing your brand effortlessly, maintaining congruence in motion, and evolving without losing your core.

Each chapter includes reflection exercises designed to help you tune your frequency with precision. These exercises are private — this is your workshop, your tuning fork, your space to be brutally honest. You're under no obligation to share this work with anyone. If you actually like the fact that you swear, then own that. I certainly do.

A Note on Language

This book is written in Australian English because that's my frequency. You'll find "realise" instead of "realize," "colour" instead of "color," and the occasional turn of phrase that might feel distinctly Down Under. This is intentional. Authenticity begins with language, and I'm not about to smooth down my voice to fit someone else's mould.

Let's Begin

Your brand is already broadcasting, whether you realise it or not. The question is: are you tuned into your authentic frequency, or are you transmitting static?

Let's find out.

You'll find lined pages for notes throughout this book. I encourage you to graffiti, doodle, and — most importantly — record your *a-HA* moments! Make it as undeniably *yours* as you can.

Jo Starling

PART ONE: FOUNDATIONS

CHAPTER 1:

THE HISTORY & PHILOSOPHY OF BRAND — FROM CATTLE TO CHARACTER

PART ONE: FOUNDATIONS

Section 1: The Cattleman's Mark

Picture this: a vast, open landscape somewhere in the Australian outback. The sun beats down on red dirt, and a mob of cattle shifts and lows in the heat as they wait their turn in the corral. At the front of the line, a fine beast is locked in the head gate. A cattleman approaches, branding iron in hand, heated to glowing in the coals of a fire. At the gate, a jackaroo deftly lops and quarterises the stumps of the horns.

The cattleman presses the iron to the hide of a steer, and the mark burns deep — a symbol, a glyph, a promise. This mark says: *These cattle belong to me. They were raised on my land, by my hand, according to my standards.*

This is where the concept of "brand" began. Not in a boardroom. Not with a logo designer. But with a searing hot iron and a need to differentiate one man's herd from another's.

At first, the brand was purely practical — a mark of ownership. But something remarkable happened over time. The brand evolved from a symbol of possession into a symbol of *reputation*.

Butchers who bought cattle from a particular pastoralist began to notice patterns. Cattle bearing certain marks consistently yielded tender, flavourful meat. Others were tougher, leaner, less desirable. The brand on the hide became a shorthand for quality — a promise that if you bought beef from *this* cattleman, you could expect *this* kind of experience.

Savvy butchers leaned into this. They'd tell their customers, "This cut is from Old Tom's herd — best beef in the district. Costs a bit more, but it's worth every penny." And customers, trusting the butcher's recommendation, would pay the premium gladly.

But here's the kicker: what happened when that promise was broken?

Imagine Old Tom, short on feed during a drought, decides to rush his cattle to market before they're properly finished. The meat that reaches the butcher's block is tougher, less marbled, disappointing. The butcher, trying to maintain his own reputation, might try to pass it off as the usual quality. Maybe he gets away with it once. Maybe twice.

But word spreads. Customers who felt cheated tell their neighbours. The butcher's reputation suffers. And Old Tom's brand — once synonymous with quality — becomes a warning instead of a promise. Trust, once broken, is almost impossible to rebuild.

This is the first lesson of branding: **a brand is a promise**. And when that promise is kept consistently, trust builds. When it's broken, trust evaporates faster than rain on a hot tin roof.

Section 2: From Cattle to Commerce — The Evolution of Brand

As commerce evolved, so did branding. The Industrial Revolution brought mass production, and with it, the need to differentiate products that were otherwise identical. A bar of soap made in Factory A needed to stand out from the bar made in Factory B, even if the ingredients were the same.

Enter the logo. The jingle. The tagline. The carefully crafted image designed to make consumers *feel* something about a product they'd never touched, made by people they'd never met.

Corporate branding became an art form. Companies like Coca-Cola, Ford, and later Apple didn't just sell products — they sold *experiences, lifestyles, identities*. The brand became bigger than the product itself. It became a promise about who you'd become if you bought in.

And it worked. Brilliantly.

But here's where things get interesting: **personal branding** has always existed, even if we didn't call it that.

Think about the village blacksmith, the local doctor, the schoolteacher, the pub owner. These people didn't have logos or marketing campaigns, but they had reputations. Their "brand" was built on their behaviour, their skill, their consistency, their character. If the blacksmith was reliable, his brand was strong. If the doctor was careless, his brand suffered — no matter how skilled he might have been.

Your behaviour was your brand. Your actions were your advertising. Your reputation was everything.

And then came the internet.

Section 3: The Digital Revolution — When Everyone Became a Brand

Before social media, most of us lived relatively private lives. Our reputations were built in small circles — family, friends, colleagues, neighbours. We could separate our "work self" from our "home self" from our "weekend self." There was room for nuance, for context, for imperfection.

Then social media swept in.

At first, it felt like Woodstock online — peace, love, and random status updates about breathing, farting, headaches, and other inane subjects. No ads. No influencers. Just mates marvelling at the digital echo chamber we'd stumbled into. We were all toddlers in a new playground, gleefully smashing buttons and figuring it out as we went.

And we made mistakes. *All of us.*

I trod on digital rakes regularly — sharing a post that didn't land, hitting "like" on something that in hindsight was off-brand (though that language didn't even exist yet), and wondering why I felt so exposed. Every misstep echoed. Not loudly, but enough to give me a creeping sense of being misaligned.

Social media provided a mirror with playback. And what it reflected back at me was a carefully costumed version of myself. I wasn't being dishonest, but I wasn't being *me* either. I was method-acting my way through early entrepreneurship, wearing a persona that I thought would sell.

I felt like a fraud. Polished and professional on the outside — but wildly incongruent on the inside.

The real me — the one with irreverent humour, blunt honesty, and a creatively chaotic brain — was buried under a mask of what I thought the world wanted.

I wasn't in alignment. And it showed.

Section 4: The Truman Show — Living in Public

THE MOMENT WE ALL BECAME BRANDS

There's a precise moment in history when personal branding stopped being optional and became essential. It wasn't when social media launched. It wasn't when smartphones put cameras in everyone's pockets. It was the moment we realised **we couldn't control the narrative anymore**.

Before the internet, you could be one person at work, another at home, and a third version at the pub on Friday night. The audiences rarely overlapped. The contexts were separate. You could code-switch between personas and no one was the wiser.

But social media collapsed all those contexts into one shared digital space. Your boss sees the same posts as your mum. Your clients can scroll through the same feed as your old school friends. The professional you and the personal you and the private you all exist in the same visible, searchable, permanent record.

This is the Truman Show. And we're all starring in it.

The question is: are you aware you're on camera? And more importantly, are you being the same person whether the red light is on or not?

WHEN "PERSONAL" STOPPED MEANING "PRIVATE"

I remember the exact moment I understood this shift. It was 2009, early days of Facebook, and I posted what I thought was a harmless joke about a frustrating client interaction (no names, no identifying details — or so I thought).

Within hours, a mutual connection had forwarded it to someone who knew exactly who I was talking about. The client saw it. The damage was done.

I hadn't broken any rules. I hadn't said anything cruel. But I'd made a critical error: **I'd assumed "personal" meant "private."**

It doesn't. Not anymore.

Every post, every like, every comment exists in a shared digital space where your audiences overlap in ways you can't predict or control. And in that space, your personal behaviour absolutely affects your business brand — whether you intend it to or not.

This isn't about living in fear. It's about living with **awareness**. Understanding that in the Truman Show, there's no backstage. There's just the show.

Here's the uncomfortable truth: **we are all living in the Truman Show now**.

Every moment is potentially being recorded, screenshot, shared. The line between "personal" and "public" has blurred to the point of non-existence. A casual Instagram story, a LinkedIn comment, a "like" on a controversial post — all of it contributes to your brand, whether you intended it to or not.

And here's the thing: **you can't turn it off**.

Even if you delete your social media accounts, your brand still exists. It lives in the minds of everyone who's ever interacted with you — online or off. It's built from the patterns they've observed, the promises you've made (spoken or unspoken), and the consistency (or lack thereof) they've experienced.

This is both terrifying and liberating.

Terrifying because there's nowhere to hide. Every interaction matters. Every post, every comment, every unguarded moment has the potential to reinforce or undermine your brand.

But liberating because once you accept this reality, you can stop performing. You can stop trying to maintain multiple versions of yourself for different audiences. You can tune into your authentic frequency and let *that* be your brand.

When you're aligned at the atomic level — when your behaviour, your values, and your public expression all match — the Truman Show stops being a threat. It becomes proof of your congruence.

Section 5: Logo vs. Brand
— The Distinction That Changes Everything

Let's clear something up right now: **your logo is not your brand**.

Your logo is a visual symbol. It's a shorthand, a marker, a piece of design. It's important, sure — but it's not your brand.

Your brand is the *promise of experience* that logo represents. It's the feeling people have when they see that symbol. It's the trust they've built (or lost) through repeated interactions with you or your business. It's the reputation that precedes you.

Think about it: when you see the Apple logo, you don't just see a piece of fruit with a bite taken out of it. You see sleek design, intuitive interfaces, premium pricing, a certain kind of aspirational lifestyle. That's brand.

When you see the Nike swoosh, you don't just see a curved line. You see athleticism, determination, victory, "Just Do It." That's brand.

The logo is the mark. The brand is the meaning attached to that mark.

And here's the critical part: *you* are your personal brand's logo. Your face, your name, your voice — these are the visual and auditory markers that represent you. But your brand is the experience people have when they encounter you.

Do they feel inspired? Intimidated? Energised? Exhausted? Confused? Connected?

That feeling — that's your brand.

And just like Old Tom's cattle mark, your personal brand is built on the promises you keep (or break) through your behaviour.

Section 6: Grandpa's Workshop — A Story of Dual Frequencies

Let me take you back in time. Back to a workshop in the Adelaide Hills, in the quiet town of Hahndorf, where your great-great-grandfather (any resemblance to actual ancestors is purely by chance) was a woodworker of great renown.

His workshop sat at the edge of town, a humble wooden structure where light streamed through a single window, dust motes dancing in the warm sunbeams. Outside, stacks of curing eucalyptus wood filled the air with their fresh, earthy scent — sharp and clean, with just a hint of honey sweetness.

Inside, the smell changed. Sawdust. Linseed oil. The faint metallic tang of hand tools. The floor was covered in wood shavings that crunched softly underfoot, and every surface bore the patina of decades of honest work.

Grandpa's reputation was built on more than his skill — it was the pride he poured into every chair and table. He carved a tiny glyph on the underside of each piece, a mark he reserved only for work that met his exacting standards. This wasn't just furniture; it was a promise.

Customers came from neighbouring towns, eager to experience the craftsmanship they'd heard about from friends who swore by Grandpa's work. The wood he used was always perfectly seasoned. The joints were seamless. The finish was so smooth you could run your hand across it and feel nothing but silk.

Imagine a woman arriving at his workshop to collect a table she'd commissioned. She's all smiles, anticipating the moment when she can trail her fingers across that silky-smooth tabletop. The exchange is as warm as the scent of eucalyptus in the air: Grandpa grins as he pulls the dust cover from the table, proud of another masterpiece. She beams back, overjoyed by her decision to invest in his work.

Both leave fulfilled — the customer with a table that exceeds her expectations, and Grandpa with his reputation intact.

This is Grandpa's frequency: meticulous, warm, generous, proud. It resonates clearly, and people tune into it with trust and delight.

But even Grandpa has his bad days.

Let's rewind and rewrite the scene.

The same woman swans into the workshop, her smile as bright as the sunlight pouring through the window. She's just as excited to pick up her table, eager to enjoy Grandpa's characteristic warmth.

But today, she isn't greeted with a grin. She's met with a scowl.

Grandpa — tired, irritable, dealing with a painful back and a splitting headache — barely looks up from his workbench. When he finally produces the table, he pushes it towards her with little ceremony, muttering something about payment.

The table itself is flawless. But the moment is soured.

The customer takes the table home, but her story changes. Instead of singing Grandpa's praises to her neighbours, she tells them about the surly craftsman who ruined her day. "The table's beautiful," she says, "but honestly, I wouldn't go back. The man was an absolutely *asshole*."

And just like that, Grandpa becomes **Grump-pa**.

Here's the critical point: Grump-pa isn't a *lie*. He's just a different facet of the same man. We all have grumpy days. We all have moments when our best selves take a back seat to exhaustion, frustration, or pain.

But in branding, **inconsistency is deadly**.

If Grump-pa becomes the dominant frequency — if customers can't predict whether they'll get the warm craftsman or the surly grouch — trust erodes. The brand promise wobbles. And eventually, people stop coming.

Unless.

Unless Grump-pa *owns* the grumpiness. Unless he leans into it, makes it part of the brand, and delivers it *consistently*.

Imagine if Grump-pa's workshop had a sign outside: "Fine Furniture by a Grumpy Old Bastard — No Small Talk, Just Quality." Imagine if his glyph wasn't a delicate flourish but a scowling face. Imagine if customers came *expecting* the gruff interaction, and left laughing about it, charmed by the audacity of a craftsman who refused to perform warmth he didn't feel.

In that scenario, Grump-pa becomes a *brand*. An authentic one. One that attracts people who appreciate his no-nonsense approach and repels those who need hand-holding.

But here's the catch: **Grump-pa must always be Grump-pa**.

If a customer encounters him at the local market one Saturday and he greets them with a warm handshake and a kind smile, the incongruence shatters trust. They'll leave confused, unsettled, wondering which version is real.

Consistency is everything.

Section 7: Barry Humphries — The Master of Managed Frequencies

Few people understood the power of consistent frequencies better than the late Sir Barry Humphries. Renowned for his iconic personas, Humphries demonstrated how multiple distinct "brands" could coexist — as long as each one maintained absolute internal consistency.

Dame Edna was a satirical whirlwind, as fabulously flamboyant as she was sharply witty. Sir Les Patterson, on the other hand, was a riot of crudeness and excess. These characters were wildly different not only from each other but also from Humphries himself, who was warm, intelligent, and composed.

What Humphries mastered was **resonance**. Dame Edna was *always* Dame Edna. Sir Les was *always* Sir Les. And Barry Humphries, the man, was a brand in his own right — distinct from the characters but never overshadowed by them.

Audiences trusted him because each persona delivered exactly what was promised. There was no bleed-through, no confusion, no incongruence. Humphries understood that you could manage multiple frequencies — as long as you never let them interfere with each other.

The lesson is clear: whether you're leaning into a persona like Grump-pa or striving to present your truest self like Grandpa, **authenticity and consistency are non-negotiable**.

A brand that honours its promise — no matter how quirky or complex — builds trust and loyalty. But when that promise falters, the brand falters with it.

Closing Reflection: Your Brand Is Already Broadcasting

Here's what I want you to understand as we close this chapter:

You already have a brand. It's broadcasting right now, in this moment. It's been broadcasting since the day you were born.

The question isn't whether you have a brand. The question is whether the brand you're broadcasting is *aligned* with who you truly are.

Are you Grandpa or Grump-pa? Or are you somewhere in between, wobbling between frequencies and wondering why people seem confused? Do you yourself feel chaotic? Manic? Exhausted by performative expressions online and off?

The work ahead — the atomic-level tuning we're about to do — will help you find your authentic frequency and amplify it with clarity and consistency. We'll strip away the static, remove the interference, and tune you back into the signal you were born to transmit.

Because the world doesn't need another carefully curated persona. It needs *you*. Your voice. Your frequency. Your truth.

Let's begin the tuning.

CHAPTER 1 EXERCISES

Exercise 1: Your Brand Archaeology

Take a moment to reflect on the "brand" you've been unconsciously broadcasting. Answer these questions honestly:

a. **What three words do you think others would use to describe you**? (Ask a trusted friend if you're not sure.)
b. **What three words do *you* want to be known for?**
c. **Where's the gap?** Are there differences between how you're perceived and how you want to be perceived? What might be causing that incongruence?
d. **Think of a time when you were "Grandpa" — when you showed up at your best and left someone feeling inspired, supported, or delighted.** What were you doing? What traits were shining through?
e. **Think of a time when you were "Grump-pa" — when you were off, tired, or not yourself, and it showed.** What happened? How did it affect the interaction?

f. **If you could claim one "Grump-pa" trait and make it part of your authentic brand** (like owning grumpiness or irreverence), **what would it be?** How might you express it consistently so it becomes a feature, not a bug?

Exercise 2: The Logo vs. Brand Distinction

Look at three brands you admire (corporate or personal). For each one:
    a. **Describe the "logo"** (the visual symbol, the name, the face).
    b. **Describe the "brand"** (the feeling, the promise, the experience people have when they encounter it).
    c. **What's one thing that brand does consistently that reinforces its promise?**

Now turn the lens on yourself:
    d. **You are your "logo." What's the promise of experience that comes with encountering you?** What do people consistently get when they interact with you?
    e. **Is that promise aligned with your authentic frequency — or is there static in the signal?**

Exercise 3: Truman Show Audit

In the age of social media, everything is potentially public. Let's do an honest audit:
    a. **Scroll through your last 20 social media posts (any platform).** Do they feel like *you*? Or do they feel like a version of you that's performing for an audience?
    b. **If a stranger scrolled your feed, what would they assume about you?** Would that assumption be accurate?
    c. **Is there anything you've posted, liked, or commented on recently that feels incongruent with the brand you want to project?** (No judgment — just awareness.)
    d. **What's one small shift you could make to bring your online presence into greater alignment with your authentic frequency?**

CHAPTER 2:

YOUR BRAND IS ALREADY AT WORK

PART ONE: FOUNDATIONS

You didn't choose to have a personal brand. It chose you the moment you were born.

From your first cry, you've been broadcasting a frequency — your temperament, your energy, your way of being in the world. Some babies are calm and observant. Others are loud and demanding. Some are easy to soothe. Others fight sleep like it's a personal affront.

These aren't flaws or virtues. They're *traits*. The raw material of your frequency.

As you grew, those traits combined with experiences, values, and choices to create **patterns**. And those patterns created *promises* — unspoken agreements about what people could expect from you.

Are you the friend who always shows up on time? That's a promise of reliability.

Are you the colleague who brings humour to tense meetings? That's a promise of levity.

Are you the family member who remembers everyone's birthday? That's a promise of care.

These promises aren't something you consciously crafted. They emerged naturally from the way you move through the world. They're your brand in motion.

And here's the thing: **your brand is working right now, whether you're managing it or not**.

Every email you send, every conversation you have, every social media post you like — it all contributes to the signal you're broadcasting. And people are tuning in, forming impressions, deciding whether you're someone they trust, admire, want to work with, or want to avoid, take seriously, or stay connected with out of morbid curiosity.

The question isn't whether you have a brand. The question is whether the brand you're broadcasting is **aligned** with who you truly are and where you're trying to go.

The Science of Pattern Recognition

HOW BRAINS BUILD BRAND IMPRESSIONS

Here's something fascinating: our brains are pattern-recognition machines. We're constantly scanning for consistency, looking for signals that tell us whether someone is trustworthy, predictable, safe.

When you interact with someone repeatedly and they show up the same way each time — same energy, same values, same general vibe — your brain files them under "reliable." Trust builds.

But when someone's behaviour is inconsistent — friendly one day, cold the next; generous in one context, stingy in another — your brain flags them as "unpredictable." Threat level rises. Trust erodes.

This isn't conscious. It's happening at a neurological level, beneath your awareness. You just know something feels "off" about that person, even if you can't articulate why.

This is why brand congruence matters so much.

Your brand — your personal frequency — is the pattern people's brains are tracking. When it's consistent, they relax. When it wavers, they tense.

And in business, that tension is the difference between "yes" and "maybe" and "no thanks."

THE 7-SECOND BRAND ASSESSMENT

Research suggests that people form first impressions in as little as seven seconds. Seven seconds.

In that tiny window, they're assessing:

- How you carry yourself (body language, energy, presence)
- How you speak (tone, vocabulary, confidence)
- How you look (not vanity — congruence between appearance and message)
- How you make them feel (safe, inspired, uncertain, uncomfortable)

And here's the kicker: **that impression is remarkably hard to shift.**

Once someone has filed you under "trustworthy" or "flaky" or "intense" or "approachable," it takes significant effort and consistent counter-evidence to change their assessment.

This is why tuning your atomic-level brand matters. Because you're not just shaping how people see you in this moment — you're shaping the lens through which they'll interpret every future interaction.

Section 1: How Brands Emerge Naturally

Your personal brand isn't something you switch on when you walk into a business meeting or post on LinkedIn. It's not a costume you put on for professional settings and shed when you get home.

Your brand is the sum total of every interaction you've ever had with another human being. It's the frequency you emit — consciously and unconsciously — in every moment.

Sometimes this works brilliantly in your favour. When you're aligned with your authentic frequency, people feel it. They're drawn to you. They trust you. They want to collaborate, connect, learn from you.

But other times, unguarded facets of your brand — the parts you're not actively managing — can undermine everything you're trying to build.

This is what I call **signal interference**. It's the static that creeps into your broadcast when you're not paying attention, creating confusion and eroding trust.

Section 2: Brian's Story — A Brand Audit in Real Life

Let me tell you about Brian.

Brian came to me several years ago when he was running for a position on the local council. He was a classic conservative middle-aged accountant: side-parted hair neatly combed with a touch of Brylcreem, lightweight business shirts (always with a singlet underneath), pressed slacks, polished shoes. He looked the part of a careful, dependable fiscal steward — exactly the image you'd want in someone managing public funds.

Brian wasn't flashy. He wasn't charismatic. But he didn't need to be. His conservative appearance and measured demeanour projected an image of caution, dependability, and fiscal responsibility — traits that would appeal to a significant portion of his electorate.

On paper, Brian's frequency was well-tuned for his goals.

But there was a problem.

As I worked with Brian, shadowing him at community events and observing his interactions, I noticed something troubling. Brian had an unguarded facet of his brand that was actively working *against* him — and he had no idea it was even there.

Brian was instinctively sexist.

Not maliciously. Not consciously. He didn't have cruel intentions or backwards beliefs. He was simply... old-fashioned. And unaware.

On any given shopping day, you could see Brian striding two steps ahead of his wife, mobile phone pressed to his ear, while she struggled behind him under the weight of six or eight shopping bags, sweat beading on her brow.

It wasn't a one-off. It was a *pattern*.

In their practice (where his wife was the Front Office Manager), Brian would interrupt her mid-sentence, talk over her, even dismiss her suggestions with a wave of his hand. Again — not out of malice. It was just ingrained behaviour, the kind that once went unquestioned in a different generation.

But the message this behaviour sent to onlookers was undeniable: *This man doesn't respect his wife.*

And if he doesn't respect his wife, what does that say about how he'll treat constituents? How he'll listen to women in the community? How he'll make decisions that affect families?

It was a branding disaster.

Without realising it, Brian was broadcasting a frequency that directly contradicted the promise he was trying to make: that he was fair, dependable, and worthy of trust.

Section 3: The Honest Conversation

Delivering this feedback to Brian was one of the hardest conversations I've ever had as a brand strategist.

How do you tell someone that their unconscious behaviour — behaviour they've probably never questioned — is sabotaging their goals?

I chose honesty. Gentle, but unflinching.

"Brian," I said over coffee one afternoon, "I need to talk to you about something you're not going to want to hear."

He looked up, startled. "Okay..."

"Your treatment of your wife is hurting your electability."

Silence.

"I don't understand," he said finally.

I explained what I'd observed. The shopping bags. The interruptions. The dismissive body language. I told him that to outside observers — particularly women voters — this behaviour suggested a lack of respect. And in an election where every vote mattered, this incongruence was costing him.

To his immense credit, Brian didn't get defensive. He was *aghast*.

"I never thought of it that way," he said quietly. "I didn't realise... I mean, that's just how we've always done things."

"I know," I said. "But intention doesn't matter if the signal you're sending says something else. Your behaviour is your brand. And right now, this part of your brand is out of tune."

He sat with that for a long moment. Then he nodded.

"What do I do?"

Section 4: Tuning the Frequency

Brian took the feedback seriously. Over the following weeks, I watched him make conscious, visible changes.

He started carrying the shopping bags. Not just some of them — *all* of them. He'd insist on it, even when his wife protested that she could manage.

He stopped interfering in front office interactions. He'd listen without interrupting. He'd acknowledge her ideas publicly and give her credit.

At community events, he'd introduce her warmly, speak about her with genuine affection and respect, and make a point of standing *beside* her rather than ahead.

The shift was profound — not just in how others perceived him, but in the relationship itself. His marriage became warmer, more visibly affectionate. His wife seemed lighter, more engaged. And the feedback from the community was immediate.

"I didn't realise how lovely Brian's wife is," one voter told me. "They make such a great team."

"He really listens to people," another said. "You can tell he respects everyone, not just the blokes."

On election day, Brian won by a landslide.

Section 5: The Lesson — Every Facet Matters

Brian's story illustrates something critical about atomic-level branding: **you can't compartmentalise your behaviour**.

You might think that how you treat your spouse in your own time has nothing to do with your professional brand. But even before the Truman Show era — where every interaction is potentially visible — your behavioural "leaks" impacted brand integrity.

Your behaviour in unguarded moments reveals your *true* frequency. It's easy to perform professionalism in a boardroom or compassion in a pitch meeting. But the way you treat the people closest to you? The way you act when you think no one important is watching?

That's your authentic frequency. And people can *feel* it, even if they can't articulate why.

Brian's conservative appearance and dependable demeanour were working for him. But his unconscious sexism was creating *static* — interference in his signal that undermined the promise he was trying to make.

Once he identified that interference and tuned it out, his frequency became clear. Consistent. Trustworthy.

And people responded.

Section 6: Patterns Create Promises

Your brand isn't built on grand gestures or carefully curated moments. It's built on **patterns** — the small, repeated behaviours that people come to rely on.

Do you always return calls within 24 hours? That's a pattern of responsiveness.

Do you show up to meetings 10 minutes early? That's a pattern of respect for others' time.

Do you remember details about people's lives and ask about them later? That's a pattern of attentiveness.

These patterns create *promises* — unspoken agreements about what people can expect from you.

And here's the critical part: **when you keep those promises consistently, trust builds. When you break them, trust erodes**.

Think about it. If you're known for always being on time, and then you start showing up late without explanation, people notice. The promise is broken. The frequency is off. And even if you have a good reason, the incongruence creates doubt.

"If they can't keep this small promise," people think, "can I trust them with bigger ones?"

This is why atomic-level branding matters. It's not about policing every moment or achieving perfection. It's about **awareness** — understanding the patterns you're creating and ensuring they align with the promises you want to make.

Section 7: Your Brand Is a Composition, Not a Solo Trait

Here's something most people misunderstand about branding: **no single trait defines you**.

Your brand is a *composition* — a unique combination of traits that interact with each other to create something greater than the sum of its parts.

Think of it like music. A single note doesn't make a song. It's the combination of notes, played together in a particular rhythm and key, that creates a melody... and one note out of place? The song is ruined.

Your personal brand works the same way.

Consider someone with a great sense of humour. On its own, that's a lovely trait. But pair it with intelligence and empathy, and it becomes *magnetic* — the kind of humour that disarms tension, builds connection, and makes people feel seen.

But pair that same sense of humour with carelessness or sarcasm, and it becomes a liability. Now you're the person who makes jokes at others' expense, who doesn't read the room, who can't be trusted with sensitive information.

Same trait. Different composition. Completely different brand.

This is why **curation** is so important. You're not inventing traits out of thin air. You're selecting which traits to amplify, which to soften, and which combinations create the resonance you're aiming for.

Section 8: The Barefoot Investor — A Masterclass in Trait Composition

Let me give you an example: Scott Pape, better known as The Barefoot Investor.

Pape has built one of the most successful personal finance brands in Australia by curating a trait composition that's both unconventional and deeply resonant with his audience.

Core Traits He Amplifies:

- **Simplicity**: Pape's advice is stripped of jargon, offering straightforward, actionable steps that anyone can follow.

No complicated formulas. No financial speak. Just clear, practical guidance.
- **Relatability**: His use of conversational language and anecdotes from his own life (often with self-deprecating humour) makes him approachable. He's not a slick banker in a suit. He's a bloke who wears thongs and talks like your mate down the pub.
- **Frugality**: His commitment to financial discipline resonates strongly with his audience. He doesn't just *teach* about living within your means — he *embodies* it.

The Unconventional Choice:

In the world of finance, most advisors lean into traits like authority, sophistication, or technical expertise. They wear expensive suits, use complex language, and position themselves as gatekeepers of knowledge.

Pape deliberately chose the opposite.

He amplified simplicity, practicality, and relatability. He made himself *accessible* rather than aspirational. And in doing so, he attracted people who felt alienated by traditional financial advice — people who wanted help, not condescension.

Living the Brand 24/7:

What makes Pape's brand particularly powerful is how well it aligns with his natural self. He doesn't need to "perform" as The Barefoot Investor. His brand is an authentic extension of his values and lifestyle.

Whether he's speaking at events, writing a book, or having a casual conversation, his patterns and promises remain consistent. This alignment ensures his brand feels effortless and believable, allowing him the freedom to embody it 24/7 without strain.

The Lesson:

Pape's success demonstrates that curating the right combination of traits isn't about following convention — it's about aligning your traits with your audience's needs and your own authenticity.

His blend of simplicity, relatability, and frugality tuned his frequency to attract a loyal, engaged tribe. And because those traits are genuinely *him*, the signal is strong, clear, and unmistakable.

Section 9: The Danger of Mismatched Traits

Not all trait combinations work. In fact, some combinations actively sabotage your brand — creating static, confusion, and distrust.

Imagine an influencer trying to dominate the party-girl space in the ladies' shoe market. A fun, savvy wit could be a perfect cornerstone trait for her brand. To amplify this, she might lean into charm, style, and playful confidence — traits that complement humour and align with her audience's aspirations.

But what if she paired that humour with recklessness? Or irresponsibility? Or mean-spirited sarcasm?

Now her brand feels *unstable*. Her audience might enjoy her content, but they wouldn't trust her. They certainly wouldn't want to associate their own reputation with hers. The humour that could have been magnetic becomes a warning sign.

This is the danger of unexamined trait composition. You might have all the right individual ingredients, but if they're combined poorly, the dish is unpalatable.

Section 10: Curating Your Trait Mix

So how do you curate the right trait mix for your brand?

It starts with **awareness**. You need to identify the traits you naturally possess, then assess how they interact with each other and with your goals.

Ask yourself:

- **What traits do I naturally amplify?** (What do people consistently notice about me?)
- **Which of those traits serve my goals?** (Do they help me build the trust, connection, or influence I'm aiming for?)
- **Which traits create static or confusion?** (Are there behaviours or patterns that contradict the promises I'm trying to make?)
- **What combinations feel authentic *and* strategic?** (What trait mix resonates with both who I am and where I'm going?)

This isn't about becoming someone you're not. It's about *tuning* — adjusting the amplitude of certain traits so your signal comes through clearly.

Think of it like a sound engineer at a mixing desk. You're not deleting tracks. You're sliding some up, bringing others down, and finding the balance that creates the most resonant sound.

Closing Reflection: Your Brand Is Already Speaking

Here's what I want you to take away from this chapter:
Your brand is already at work. Right now. In this moment.

Every pattern you've established, every promise you've made (spoken or unspoken), every trait you've amplified — it's all broadcasting a frequency that others are tuning into.

The question is: **are you managing that frequency intentionally, or is it managing you?**

Brian's story shows us that even unconscious behaviours contribute to our brand. The way we treat people when we think no one important is watching. The small habits we've never questioned. The trait combinations we've never examined.

All of it matters.

But here's the good news: once you become *aware* of the frequency you're broadcasting, you can tune it. You can identify the static, adjust the amplitude, and create a signal that's clear, consistent, and aligned with your authentic self.

That's the work we're doing together. That's atomic-level branding.
And we're just getting started.

CHAPTER 2 EXERCISES

Before we begin these exercises, let's revisit the difference between traits and patterns. *Traits* are your "as-born settings" — your baseline temperament, characteristics, and energy: the way you are before you've learned strategies, masks, roles, or "how to be." *Patterns*, on the other hand, are the "loops that form" when those traits meet life. They're the consistent behaviours that emerge as you grow — the repetitions people come to recognise, rely on, and predict because they keep showing up.

Exercise 1: **Pattern** Recognition

Think about the patterns you've established in your professional and personal life. Answer these questions:

a. **What are three patterns people have come to expect from you?** (Always on time? Always bringing snacks to meetings? Always available for late-night texts?)

b. **What promises do those patterns create?** (Reliability? Generosity? Accessibility?)

c. **Are there any patterns you've established that you *don't* want to be known for?** (Always saying yes even when you're overwhelmed? Always being the one who organises everything?)

d. **If you could establish one *new* pattern starting today, what would it be?** (And what promise would it create?)

Exercise 2: The "Grandpa vs. Grump-pa" Audit

Reflect on your own behaviour in different contexts:
a. **Describe a recent "Grandpa" moment** — when you showed up at your best and left someone feeling valued, inspired, or supported. What traits were you amplifying?
b. **Describe a recent "Grump-pa" moment** — when you were off, tired, or not yourself, and it showed in your behaviour. What happened? How do you think it affected your brand?
c. **Is there a "Grump-pa" trait that could serve you if you own it and make it consistent**? How might you do that authentically?

Exercise 3: **Trait** Composition Analysis

Let's examine how your traits work together. You need to **feel** into your traits. Are you already curating these due to perceived expectations? Could you feel more congruent if you leant into curated traits differently?
a. **List five traits that people consistently notice about you.** (Ask trusted friends if you're not sure.)
b. **For each trait, identify a "complementary trait" that enhances it** and a "conflicting trait" that would undermine it.
Example:
 - Trait: Sense of humour
 - Complementary: Intelligence (makes humour sharp and insightful)
 - Conflicting: Carelessness (makes humour feel reckless or hurtful)
c. **Looking at your current trait mix, are there any combinations that might be creating static or confusion?** What could you adjust?
d. **What's one trait you could amplify more intentionally to strengthen your brand?**

Exercise 4: The Unspoken Promise Inventory

Your brand makes promises every day, whether you intend to or not. Let's identify them:
- a. **Based on your patterns of behaviour, what do you think people expect from you?**
- b. **Are those expectations aligned with the promises you *want* to make?**
- c. **Is there a promise you've been making unconsciously that you'd like to change?** (For example: always being available, even at the expense of your own wellbeing?)
- d. **What's one small action you could take this week to begin reshaping that promise?**

PART TWO: TUNING YOUR FREQUENCY

CHAPTER 3:

BRANDING AS SELF-EXPRESSION

Imagine standing in front of a blank canvas, paintbreush in hand. There are no instructions, no rules, just infinite potential. Every choice — every brushstroke, colour, texture — comes from you. This is the essence of atomic-level branding: a deeply personal act of self-expression that tells the world who you are, what you stand for, and why you matter.

Too often, we think of branding as something manufactured — slick logos, clever taglines, curated personas. But true, magnetic brands aren't created in boardrooms or Photoshop. They're born from within, shaped by your quirks, values, and the unique ways you interpret the world.

Your Atomic-Level Brand (ALB) isn't a costume you wear for others. It's an extension of your creativity and purpose, woven into the way you solve problems, tell stories, and connect with people. And the more you lean into the traits that make you *you*, the more your brand resonates with authenticity and power.

In this chapter, we'll explore how your natural creativity shapes your brand, why emotional and instinctive connections matter more than polish, and how standing out isn't about trying harder — it's about being more of yourself.

Because the world doesn't need another copy of someone else's success. It needs the original version of you.

Creativity as Your Competitive Advantage

WHY COOKIE-CUTTER BRANDS FAIL

Let me tell you what doesn't work: copying someone else's brand.

I see it all the time. Someone admires a successful entrepreneur — let's call her Sarah. Sarah's brand is warm, accessible, storytelling-focused. She built a massive following by sharing vulnerable personal anecdotes and connecting deeply with her audience.

So a new entrepreneur thinks, "I'll do that too!" They start mimicking Sarah's tone, her structure, her themes. They post vulnerable stories because that's what Sarah does.

But it feels forced. Hollow. Off.

Because they're not Sarah. Their frequency is different. Their stories are different. Their natural mode of expression is different.

And their audience can feel it. The mimicry creates **dissonance** — a mismatch between the signal they're broadcasting and the frequency they actually carry.

The result? No one tunes in. Or worse, people tune in initially but leave when they sense the inauthenticity.

This is why atomic-level branding starts with your own raw material. Not someone else's blueprint. Not an industry template. *Your* traits, *your* stories, *your* voice.

Because the only way to be truly magnetic is to broadcast a frequency that's genuinely yours.

THE HIDDEN COST OF SUPPRESSED CREATIVITY

When you suppress your creative instincts — when you smooth down your quirks, hide your unconventional perspectives, or force yourself into someone else's mould — something happens.

You lose energy.

Not just metaphorically. Literally. The cognitive load of maintaining a persona that doesn't match your natural frequency is exhausting. It drains your capacity for genuine creative work. It makes everything feel harder than it should.

But when you lean into your authentic creative frequency — when you let yourself express ideas in your natural style, tell stories in your natural voice, solve problems in your natural way — **energy flows**.

Work feels lighter. Ideas come faster. Connection happens more easily.

This is the hidden gift of atomic-level branding: it doesn't just make you more magnetic to others. It makes you more energised for yourself

Section 1: Creativity as Your Brand's Wellspring

We often associate creativity with artists, musicians, or designers. But creativity isn't limited to the arts — it's the lens through which you see the world and solve problems.

Creativity is how you approach challenges. It's the story you tell when someone asks what you do. It's the way you connect disparate ideas into something new. It's the humour you bring to tense situations, the metaphors you use to explain complex concepts, the perspective that makes people think, "I never thought of it that way."

Your creativity is already shaping your brand/s — whether you realise it or not.

Think about it: when you solve a problem in an unconventional way, you're expressing creativity. When you reframe a setback as an opportunity, you're expressing creativity. When you find a unique angle on a tired topic, you're expressing creativity.

This creative expression becomes part of your frequency. It's what makes you memorable, relatable, and distinct.

Section 2: Art School Froze Me — A Personal Story

For me, the power — and danger — of stifling creativity became crystal clear at art school.

I was born creative. I'm a naturally gifted artist. Not bragging. Just fact. It's a facet of my frequency I lean into. My entire life is built upon it.

So when I left school early to take up an offer to study Fine Art at university, I thought I was stepping into my zone of genius. I was excited. Terrified, but excited.

But instead of flourishing, I ran into something unexpected: my own conformity.

Despite loving expressive, abstract artists like John Olsen and Joan Miró, I found myself frozen. My lecturers urged me to "loosen up," to be raw and experimental — but I couldn't do it. I had technical skill, yes, but artistic freedom had become a demon I didn't know how to wrestle.

After more than a few tearful studio critiques, I realised the culprit: **school had taught me to seek approval instead of expression.**

I'd been top of my art class for years, praised for my ability to render perfect perspective and fine detail. Because when art becomes part of a graded curriculum, creativity is no longer enough — you must be *measurably good.* So what gets rewarded? Technical accuracy. Neat shading. Clean lines. Conformity.

In chasing top marks, I'd sanded back my own edge. I'd traded expression for approval. I was polished to perfection — and completely disconnected from the raw, chaotic creativity that had drawn me to art in the first place.

The irony wasn't lost on me. I'd been *branded* by the education system as a "good artist" — and in the process, lost access to the very thing that made art matter to me.

Section 3: The Demon I Dance With

Today, I've learned to love the tension between chaos and control. That juxtaposition is now what I paint. It's the dance I tread with my old demon. And it's where my truest brand shines through.

I don't shy away from technical skill — I use it deliberately. But I've also reclaimed the freedom to let paint drip, to leave edges rough, to embrace the accidents that make a piece feel *alive.*

That balance — between precision and wildness — has become my signature. It's authentically *me*. And it only emerged when I stopped trying to be what I thought I should be and started tuning back into my natural frequency.

This is the essence of atomic-level branding: reclaiming the parts of yourself that were smoothed down, dulled, or buried under layers of expectation.

Your brand becomes powerful not when you add more polish, but when you strip away what's inauthentic and let your raw creative frequency resonate.

Section 4: My Daughter's Native Rawness

As a mother of a highly intelligent and creative daughter, my personal experience with societal sculpting steeled my resolve to protect her from the same limiting forces.

I didn't teach her to draw.

That might sound odd coming from someone whose life is built on visual creativity, but it was intentional. I wanted her to explore her own creative frequency without my influence shaping it.

And she still drew feverishly! Gorgeous, succinct, expressive line drawings that somehow managed to capture every subject perfectly, with a kind of **native rawness** that just made me drool. As a proud mum, I celebrated every piece (and still have them).

Funnily enough, as my young woman grew through her schooling, she developed a bit of resentment towards me for taking this position. She wanted my skills. She wanted the technical training I'd deliberately withheld.

Of course, I apologised and explained why I had held back my knowledge, and then set about making art camps for us. We spent weekends together learning techniques, experimenting with mediums, pushing each other's skills.

As she fervently explores developing her rendering skills now, I'm struck by the contrast in our desires. She craves the technical mastery I have. I crave the raw freedom she once embodied.

It's highlighted to me the importance of recognising that **we are absolutely all one-offs**.

There is no single "right" frequency. No universal brand template. The work isn't about becoming what someone else values — it's about understanding what *you* need to express your truest self.

My daughter needed technique to feel free. I needed freedom to feel authentic. Same creative drive. Opposite approaches. Both valid.

Section 5: Society Prefers Beige (But It's Not My Favourite Colour)

From the moment we begin to interact with the world, we're shaped — intentionally or otherwise — by expectations, norms, and judgements. Over time, we adapt, cover up, conform. It's a natural response to schooling, society, and survival.

You weren't born beige. Society, however, prefers us to be so. For my part, **it's not my favourite colour**.

But things are shifting. With increasing awareness and acceptance of neurodivergence and the sheer breadth of human diversity, we're witnessing a long-overdue celebration of uniqueness. And this isn't just welcome news for the neurodivergent community — it's an invitation to all of us to reflect.

To reflect on what may have been dulled or smoothed down over time... and to reclaim it.

Somewhere along the way, many of us have been bogged and puttied, sanded smooth and "coated in the blandness of beige" by the pressure to conform. School systems, social norms, cultural cues — all applying layer after layer of that safe-toned enamel. The traits that made us vibrant, expressive, or unpredictable got glazed over to fit into a monochrome and predictable social panorama.

But underneath that enamel? Your fabulous one-of-a-kind frequency lies waiting to be uncovered.

Atomic-level branding invites us to pick up the chisel and grinder... and begin revealing it!

Section 6: Unearthing What's Been Buried

The experiences that chip away at your expression don't remove your uniqueness. They just suppress it. Outside forces only ever smooth surfaces by filling in the divots. **Only you have control of the true form.**

The real you is still there. And the more of that raw material you can unearth, the more authentic, distinctive, and powerful your brand will be.

Of course, you'll find traits that won't serve you well. We all have those! But it's *you* who chooses which to lean into, and which to sand down.

As you work through this chapter, I hope you find some demons of your own to dance with.

Section 7: Emotional and Instinctive Connections

Think back to the last time you felt an instant connection with a brand or a person. Maybe it was a product that made you feel understood, or a story that stirred something deep inside you. These moments of connection aren't random — they're **emotional and instinctive**. And they're the cornerstone of powerful personal branding.

When your brand reflects who you truly are, it resonates with others on a level that goes beyond logic. People are drawn to authenticity because it feels real, trustworthy, and relatable. It's not just about what you say or do — it's about how you make people *feel*.

People rarely make decisions purely based on logic. Studies show that our brains process emotional responses faster than rational thoughts. In branding, this means your audience is often deciding how they feel about you before they've even had time to think about it. Authenticity amplifies this emotional response, creating trust and relatability.

Section 8: Miriam Margolyes — Unfiltered and Unforgettable

Let me give you an example: Miriam Margolyes.

Miriam is a perfect illustration of a personal brand that connects emotionally and instinctively. While she's had a long career as an actress, it's her later-life reinvention that has turned her into a global phenomenon. Her secret? **Embracing the traits that make her unapologetically herself.**

Margolyes has leaned into her unfiltered honesty, sharp humour, and candidness about personal topics. Whether she's sharing a cheeky anecdote about her love life or railing against social injustices, she exudes a raw authenticity that makes people feel like they truly *know* her. Her ability to balance humour and vulnerability allows her audience to see her as both larger-than-life and deeply relatable.

The Outcome:

Miriam Margolyes' brand doesn't rely on glossy perfection or scripted performances. Instead, it thrives on the authenticity of her personality, which creates emotional bonds with her audience. Her story shows how being unfiltered and embracing your quirks can elevate your personal brand in ways that feel effortless.

Lesson:

When you amplify traits that feel true to who you are, your brand naturally becomes more emotionally resonant and magnetic.

Section 9: Trust Is the Ultimate Currency

In today's world, trust and believability aren't just desirable — they're essential.

With the rise of internet scams, phishing emails, deepfakes, and AI-generated content, people have become more guarded than ever. Our "spidey-senses" are on high alert, instinctively scanning every piece of content and communication for signs of incongruence. A single misstep — an email that feels "off," a brand statement that doesn't align with actions — can erode trust instantly.

Why This Matters for Your Brand/s:

As technology evolves, people are becoming more skilled at detecting inauthenticity. They can spot when a smile doesn't reach the eyes, when a story feels contrived, or when a promise goes unfulfilled. This makes authenticity, dependability, and congruence more valuable than ever before.

Your audience isn't just looking for a product or service — they're looking for someone they can *believe in*.

How to Stand Out:

By leaning into your authentic traits and consistently delivering on your promises, you create an ALB that feels human, not manufactured. This authenticity sets you apart in a world where scepticism is growing. Your realness becomes your superpower, drawing in people who value honesty and reliability.

Section 10: Standing Out by Being More You

The phrase "standing out" often conjures images of flashy marketing tactics, loud voices, or gimmicks designed to grab attention. But here's the truth: **real differentiation isn't about shouting the loudest or reinventing the wheel. It's about being more of who you already are**.

The more authentically you lean into your unique traits, the more naturally you attract the people who resonate with you.

Standing out isn't a performance. It's a deep alignment between your identity, your audience, and your goals. When you amplify the qualities that make you distinctive, you stop trying to fit into someone else's mould and instead define a space that's entirely your own.

Section 11: The Power of Quirks

Your quirks — the things that make you "different" — are often the very qualities that make you memorable. While it's tempting to try to smooth over imperfections or conceal idiosyncrasies, those quirks are where your brand's authenticity shines through. They make you human, relatable, and unforgettable.

Remember Scott Pape, The Barefoot Investor? He built his brand by leaning into traits that are both unconventional and deeply relatable. His no-nonsense approach to finance, coupled with an unpolished, conversational style, turned what could have been a dry subject into a movement.

He didn't aim to be the most polished financial guru — he aimed to be the most *real*. By amplifying his everyday persona and making finance accessible, Pape created a brand that feels approachable, authentic, and utterly unique.

Lesson:

Perfection doesn't connect; humanity does. When you lean into your quirks, you not only stand out but also build a brand that's impossible to replicate.

Section 12: Tuning Your Personal Brand Magnet

Let's return to an earlier metaphor: your personal brand as a magnet with two poles. One pole attracts your ideal audience, while the other repels those who don't align with your values or purpose.

This polarity isn't a flaw; it's a strength.

A strong brand isn't for everyone — it's for *your tribe*. The people who resonate with your frequency, who value what you offer, who trust your promises.

To tune your magnet effectively, you need to understand your audience and be clear on your objectives. Who are you trying to reach? What do you want to achieve?

When combined effectively, your chosen traits form the blueprint of your unique brand magnet, attracting the people who resonate most with your message and repelling those who don't.

And that's exactly what you want.

Because trying to appeal to everyone dilutes your signal. It creates static. It makes your frequency muddy and unclear, like a poorly tuned radio.

But when you tune into your authentic frequency and amplify it with clarity, you create a signal so strong, so distinct, that your people can't help but tune in.

Section 13: Leaning Into Your Differentiators

In a crowded marketplace, the key to differentiation isn't trying to be everything to everyone — it's **doubling down on the things that make you singular.**

This doesn't mean ignoring weaknesses or challenges; it means choosing which traits to amplify and which to refine.

Example: Tee Is For Todd

Consider television personality and advertising guru, Todd Sampson. Australians will know of Todd as a panellist on the ABC series of Gruen (in its various iterations) and through his great documentaries. He's the Canadian-born creative in the graphic tee-shirt (Am I the only person who wonders whether: a) he designs each one specifically for the episode, and; b) is there a cryptic message for those who spend the time to cypher it out?). Every other guest, panellist and presenter is in their corporate wear — Todd is comfortably *Todd*.

If I were to engage Leo-Burnett as my advertising agency (Todd is the CEO at the time of writing) and bumped into a suit-clad Todd in the corridors, I'd be devastated. I'd feel I'd been duped by a public persona. I would be unlikely to take him on his word, going forward. So powerful is his brand.

Todds quirky and curiosity-provoking tees add personality to his brand without overshadowing his credibility. In fact, they have earned greater rapport from me than any of the other regulars. It's a signature trait, making him memorable and approachable in a competitive and often elitist field.

Lesson:

Your greatest differentiators may be things you've been taught to downplay, or traits that others shy away from. By embracing them thoughtfully, you not only stand out but also create a powerful brand, entirely your own.

Closing Reflection: The Secret to Standing Out

Here's what I want you to take away from this chapter:

The secret to standing out isn't trying harder — it's **leaning deeper**.

By tuning your brand to your natural strengths, quirks, and creative instincts, you create something magnetic, sustainable, and deeply personal. The world doesn't need more copies or imitations. It needs your voice, your perspective, and your authenticity.

When you embrace who you are — flaws, quirks, and all — you don't just stand out. You create a brand that's impossible to forget.

In the next chapter, we'll dive into the work of identifying and refining your traits at the atomic level — chiselling away what doesn't serve you and polishing what makes you shine.

Let's get to work.

PART TWO: TUNING YOUR FREQUENCY

CHAPTER 3 EXERCISES

Exercise 1: Chipping Out the Bog

Objective: Identify traits that have been panel-beaten, bogged and "beiged" by societal expectations and reclaim them.

    a. **What parts of your personality were most celebrated as a child?**

Consider the traits you were praised for — enthusiasm, creativity, helpfulness, focus, humour. Which of these were authentic to you, and which were behaviours you learned to maintain approval?

    b. **Which traits were quietly — or not so quietly — discouraged?**
Were you told to be "less much"? Too loud, too sensitive, too silly, too serious? These are the traits society often paints over. List a few that you think might have been "beiged."

    c. **Are there traits you've hidden due to shame or fear of judgement?**
Traits like being opinionated, irreverent, eccentric, or even deeply emotional might be exactly what sets your brand apart — if you have the courage to embrace them.

    d. **Choose one "beiged" trait you're ready to reclaim.**
How might you express it authentically in your brand? What would it look like to lean into this trait rather than suppress it?

Exercise 2: Creative Expression Audit

Objective: Identify how your natural creativity already shapes your brand.
- a. **Think of a recent problem you solved in an unconventional way.** What was the problem? How did you approach it differently than others might have?
- b. **What's a metaphor or story you use often to explain complex ideas?** Why does it resonate with you? What does it reveal about your creative lens?
- c. **When do you feel most creatively alive?** What are you doing? Who are you with? How might you bring more of that energy into your ALB?
- d. **Is there a creative pursuit you've abandoned or suppressed?** (Writing, music, design, cooking, gardening, etc.) What would it look like to integrate that creativity back into your life — and your ALB?

Exercise 3: Emotional Connection Map

Objective: Understand how you make people *feel*.
- a. **Think of three people who seem drawn to you or your work.** What do you think attracts them? What feeling do you evoke in them?
- b. **Now think of three people who seem resistant or indifferent to your brand.** Why might that be? (Remember: repelling the wrong people is just as important as attracting the right ones.)
- c. **How do you want your dream tribe to feel when they encounter your brand?**
  (Inspired? Comforted? Energised? Challenged? Seen? Empowered?)
- d. **What's one small action you could take this week to amplify that feeling in your interactions?**

Exercise 4: The Quirk Inventory

Objective: Identify and embrace your quirks.

    a. **List three "quirks" or unconventional traits you possess.** (Things you do differently, perspectives you hold, habits that set you apart.)

    b. **For each quirk, ask:**
- Do I suppress this or lean into it?
- How might this quirk strengthen my brand if I expressed it more openly?
- Is there a way to express this quirk that feels authentic *and* aligned with my goals?

    c. **Choose one quirk to amplify intentionally this month.** How will you do it?

CHAPTER 4:

TUNING YOUR FREQUENCY — IDENTIFYING AND REFINING YOUR TRAITS

Your traits are your raw material.

Not every trait will be one you love, and not every trait will serve your goals. But when you start identifying, sorting, and refining these traits, you begin to consciously shape your ALB from the inside out.

Think of your personal brand as a **frequency that needs tuning**. All the raw material is already there — the unique combination of personality traits, habits, instincts, and quirks that make you *you*. And the pressure you've experienced throughout your life — challenges, grief, growth — isn't wasted. It's what forged your frequency in the first place, like a diamond in the rough.

But you are not going to be the first to tune your frequency. **Life itself tuned you first.**

From the moment we begin to interact with the world, we're shaped — intentionally or otherwise — by expectations, norms, and judgements. Over time, we adapt, cover up, conform. It's a natural response to schooling, society, and survival.

But here's the good news: underneath all that adaptation, your authentic frequency is still broadcasting. You just need to learn to hear it clearly again.

This chapter is about doing that work — identifying the traits that make up your frequency, sorting them into what serves you and what creates static, and then beginning the process of tuning your signal with precision and intention.

Section 1: Your Traits Aren't Good or Bad — They're Yours

Before we go any further, let's establish something critical: **traits aren't inherently good or bad**.

A trait that doesn't serve you in one context might be pure gold in another. Stubbornness, for example, could be reframed as determination. Sensitivity could be emotional intelligence. Bluntness could be refreshing honesty.

The work of atomic-level branding isn't about judging yourself. It's about **awareness and curation**.

You're not trying to become someone else. You're trying to understand which traits to amplify, which to soften, and which combinations create the clearest, most resonant signal.

Section 2: Prospecting for Hidden Gems — A Personal Example

I've always had the ability to intuitively feel others' needs and project back exactly what they need to hear. It's not psychic — I'm not reading minds — but it often feels just as potent. My insights are usually spot on. People often tell me that I've articulated something they didn't even know they needed clarity on.

It's an incredible gift. But not a gift that always felt like one.

This same trait made me adaptable, responsive, and incredibly in tune with my environment. It's why, throughout high school, my friends gravitated towards me for guidance and support. They called me **wise beyond my years**. I was the go-to confidant, the deep thinker, the one who could hold space and make sense of chaos.

But at home, this wasn't celebrated.

I was told I was **fickle**. That my insights shifted too fast, my ideas changed too often. It stung.

Now, with adult hindsight, I can see what was really happening. My adaptability was being misunderstood. My natural reflex to tune into others and adjust accordingly — like a radio dial finding the clearest station — was being read as inconsistency.

But it wasn't inconsistency. It was **responsiveness**. And today, I lean into it.

It's one of the most powerful facets of my personal brand. It's why my work resonates so deeply. I don't deliver copy-and-paste insights — I meet people where they are. And I grow every time I do it.

Brand Insight:

Traits that have been buried, criticised, or misunderstood often hold the most creative potential. Don't just polish what's visible — prospect for what's been hidden.

Section 3: The Camera Used to Terrify Me

For years, I was terrified of being on camera.

This might surprise you, given that I now coach people on personal branding and digital presence. But it's true. The lens made me freeze. My mind would go blank. My carefully crafted thoughts would scatter like startled birds.

I tried to present myself as earnest and authoritative — serious, knowledgeable, composed. But the camera saw right through me. What came across wasn't the confident mentor I wanted to be, but someone self-conscious and uncertain.

It wasn't working. At all.

Then I took a step back and reflected on my innate strengths. I realised that **storytelling is second nature to me**, and my **self-effacing sense of humour** is one of my most disarming traits.

So I decided to lean into these qualities instead.

Now, I don't use scripts; I use notes. I let myself tell stories, even if I waffle a bit, because it keeps the tone conversational and natural.

I engage with my audience as if I'm chatting with a friend over coffee. The transformation has been profound.

Not only does this approach feel far more authentic to me, but feedback from my audience has reinforced the value of this shift. They find me funny, engaging, and insightful. They feel *connected* to me, not lectured by me.

This realignment of my presentation style with my personal frequency is what I mean by **atomic-level branding**.

I didn't add anything new to myself — I simply refined the traits I already had, turning down the amplitude on "earnest authority" and turning up the amplitude on "conversational storytelling."

And in doing so, I found my voice.

Section 4: Sorting Traits
— What to Amplify, Keep, or Release

As we move from awareness to refinement, it's time to begin **sorting**.

Create a working document — one you'll return to throughout this book — to help you sort your traits into three categories:

1. POLISHABLE FACETS

Traits with potential to strengthen your authenticity and align with your goals. These are the traits you want to lean into, turn up, broadcast more clearly.

2. CORE TRAITS

Essential, unchanging traits that keep you grounded and consistent. These are the bedrock of your frequency — the traits that define you no matter what context you're in.

3. CAST-OFFS

Traits or habits that hold you back or contradict your brand promise. These might be patterns you've absorbed from others, behaviours that no longer serve you, or tendencies that create static in your signal.

Section 5: Seed Examples to Get You Started

Let me give you some examples to help you think about this process:

POLISHABLE FACETS:
- Storytelling ability: "I can turn everyday moments into compelling narratives. I want to use this more intentionally in my content."
- Empathy: "I naturally tune into what others need. I could lean into this in client relationships and team leadership."
- Irreverent humour: "I've been hiding this, but it's actually one of my most magnetic traits. Time to own it."

CORE TRAITS:
- Integrity: "I can't compromise on honesty, even when it's uncomfortable. This is non-negotiable."
- Curiosity: "I'm always asking 'why' and exploring new ideas. This drives everything I do."
- Resilience: "I bounce back from setbacks. This is part of my DNA."

CAST-OFFS:
- People-pleasing: "I've learned to say yes to everything, even when it drains me. This pattern needs to go."
- Perfectionism: "It's been paralysing me. I need to let go of needing everything to be flawless before I share it."
- Over-apologising: "I apologise for things that aren't my fault. This undermines my authority."

\

Section 6: This Is a Living Document

Here's something important: **this list will evolve**.

Your awareness will sharpen. Your goals will shift. Traits you once thought were liabilities might reveal themselves as strengths. Behaviours you've clung to might no longer serve you.

That's exactly the point.

This document becomes your blueprint — a filter for decisions, opportunities, content, and self-assessment. As we move through the next chapters, you'll use it to further refine your voice and ensure every outward expression is aligned with your true frequency.

Revisit it often. Adjust as you grow. Let it be a reflection of your ongoing tuning process.

Section 7: The Fickle vs. Wise Reframe

Let me return to my own example for a moment, because it illustrates something crucial about trait reframing.

The same trait — my responsiveness and adaptability — was labelled differently depending on the context:

- At home: **Fickle** (negative)
- At school: **Wise** (positive)

Same trait. Different interpretation. Completely different impact on my self-perception.

For years, I internalised the "fickle" label. I saw my adaptability as a flaw, something to hide or suppress. But when I reframed it as **responsiveness** — a trait that allows me to meet people where they are and offer exactly what they need — it became one of my greatest assets.

This is the power of reframing.

When you can look at a trait that's been criticised or misunderstood and see its hidden value, you unlock new potential. You take control of the narrative. You decide what that trait means and how it serves you.

Ask yourself: **What trait have I been told is "too much" or "not enough" that might actually be my secret weapon?**

Section 8: Anger Management
— A Trait I Don't Love, But I Manage

Let me be brutally honest with you about a trait I don't particularly like about myself: **I suffer from blind fury.**

It's not something I'm proud of. It's not a trait that aligns well with my personal brand of empathy, wisdom, and thoughtful guidance. But it's *there*. It's part of my frequency.

If I denied or shunned this part of myself, it would hold power over me, waiting to erupt at the worst moment and damage my carefully refined brand like a termite gnawing through whatever stands in its path.

But by **acknowledging this trait and the risk it poses to my brand**, I've built systems to manage it.

When I sense anger rising, my personal brand takes over and steers me towards a more measured response. I pause. I breathe. I choose my words carefully. I don't suppress the anger entirely — that would be inauthentic — but I tune the *expression* of it so it doesn't create static.

This is the diligence that personal branding at the atomic level demands.

It's not a matter of perfection — it's about having the self-awareness to take control of traits that could otherwise sabotage your efforts.

Section 9: Swearing as Artful Punctuation

On the flip side, there's a trait I used to hide that I now fully own: **I swear**.

Not constantly. Not carelessly. But deliberately. I use swearing as **artful punctuation** — a way to add emphasis, humour, and rawness to my storytelling (Anyone else a fan of the one-of human, Billy Connolly?).

For years, I thought I couldn't swear if I wanted to be taken seriously. I thought professionalism meant polished, sanitised language.

But here's the truth: when I swear, it's *authentic*. It's part of my voice. And in the right context, it's not only acceptable — it's magnetic.

I'm not suggesting you should swear if it doesn't feel natural to you. But I *am* suggesting that if there's a part of your authentic voice you've been suppressing because you think it's "unprofessional" or "inappropriate," you might want to reconsider.

Curation doesn't mean censorship. It means choosing *when* and *how* to express traits, not whether they exist.

Section 10: The PTSD Revelation — Shattering the Crystal Curtain

Here's a story I don't often share, but it's one of the most profound moments of brand clarity I've ever experienced.

For years, I carried undiagnosed PTSD. I didn't realise it — I just thought I was resilient, highly empathetic, a bit intense. But the trauma was there, quietly shaping my behaviour, my relationships, my worldview.

When I was recently diagnosed and began to address it, something remarkable happened. It was like **shattering a crystal curtain I'd been wearing like a muumuu** — something I'd wrapped myself in without realising how much it was distorting the light.

The day I embraced my PTSD, stood in it, and spoke about it openly, everything changed.

From that position of frank vulnerability, others suddenly understood my deep empathy and wisdom. It was like a font of resonance and relatability that lent clarity to all my stories. My insights, my emotional intelligence, my ability to hold space for others — it all made *sense* in the context of what I'd lived through.

When I stopped trying to insist I was strong and wise — and instead just dropped the bullshit and said, "here, judge for yourself" — my stories started to land.

This is the power of standing in your truth.

When you no longer need to announce your worth or perform your polish, the signal gets clearer. Magnetism builds not from creating a brand persona, but from chipping away everything that's not true.

Closing Reflection: The Work of Tuning

Here's what I want you to take away from this chapter:

Your frequency is made up of traits — some you love, some you tolerate, some you'd rather not have. But they're all *yours*.

The work of atomic-level branding isn't about becoming perfect. It's about becoming **clear**.

It's about identifying which traits to amplify, which to keep as foundations, and which to release. It's about reframing traits that have been misunderstood and owning traits you've been told to hide.

It's about building systems to manage the traits that don't serve you and creating space to express the ones that do.

And most importantly, it's about doing this work with **brutal honesty** — because you're under no obligation to share it with anyone else. This is your private tuning process. Your workshop. Your frequency to refine.

In the next chapter, we'll explore how to align your tuned frequency with reality — ensuring that what you broadcast matches who you are, even in the Truman Show era where everything is visible.

Let's keep tuning.

CHAPTER 4 EXERCISES

Exercise 1: Trait Sorting — Your First Draft

Create three lists using the framework you've created:
Polishable Facets:
List 3-5 traits you want to lean into more intentionally.
Core Traits:
List 3-5 unchanging traits that define who you are.
Cast-Offs:
List 3-5 traits or patterns you're ready to let go of.
Remember: This is a living document. You'll revisit and revise it as your awareness grows.

Exercise 2: The Reframe Exercise

Think of a trait you've been criticised for or told is "too much."
a. **What's the trait?**
b. **How was it labelled negatively?**
c. **How could you reframe it as a strength?**
d. **How might this reframed trait serve your brand?** (Note: not all will reframe positively. That's to be accepted.)

Example:
- Trait: Being very direct and blunt
- Negative label: "Too harsh" or "Abrasive"
- Reframe: "Refreshingly honest" or "Cuts through the bullshit"
- Brand value: People trust that I'll tell them the truth, even when it's uncomfortable

Exercise 3: Hidden Gem Inventory

Reflect on traits that were valued in one context but dismissed in another (like my "fickle" vs. "wise" experience).
a. **What's a trait that was celebrated in one area of your life but criticised in another?**
b. **Which interpretation felt more true to you?**
c. **How might you reclaim or lean into this trait now?**

Exercise 4: Managing the Traits You Don't Love

Be honest: **What's one trait you have that doesn't align well with your brand goals?**
a. **Describe the trait.**
b. **How does it create static or undermine your promises?**
c. **What system could you build to manage it?** (Like my anger management awareness)
d. **Can this trait be tuned rather than eliminated?**

POLISHABLE FACETS	CORE TRAITS	CAST-OFFS

CHAPTER 5:

ALIGNING YOUR RESONANCE WITH REALITY

In Chapter 1, we explored the roots of branding — that a brand is, at its essence, a promise. A signal to others of what to expect from us, whether it's the tender meat from a cattleman's herd or the warmth of a well-crafted customer experience.

But when we shift our focus from business brand to personal brand, something changes. The notion of a "promise" can feel a little stiff. Personal branding isn't contractual; it's relational. Emotional. Lived.

Which is why, throughout this chapter, we'll move away from the idea of "brand promise" and instead embrace a more human, dynamic concept: **Resonance**.

The Ripple Effects of Incongruence

HOW SMALL LEAKS CREATE BIG PROBLEMS

You don't lose trust in one dramatic moment. You lose it in tiny increments — micro-betrayals so small you might not even notice them happening.

A promise you didn't quite keep.

A value you compromised just this once.

A behaviour that contradicted what you said you stood for.

A post you liked that didn't quite align with your brand.

Each one, on its own, is negligible. But they accumulate. They create a pattern. And patterns create expectations.

This is how incongruence erodes trust: slowly, quietly, almost invisibly — until suddenly it's obvious.

I watched this happen to a colleague once. She built a beautiful brand around "authentic leadership" and "collaborative decision-making." Her content was inspiring. Her workshops were transformative.

But behind the scenes, she was autocratic. Dismissive of input. Quick to take credit, slow to give it. Her team lived it. Her clients eventually saw it. And one by one, they stopped believing the brand. Her business failed.

Not because her product was flawed or she did anything *dramatically* wrong. But because the small, daily behaviours didn't match the big, public promises.

Atomic-level branding demands congruence at every level — especially the levels you think don't matter.

Section 1: Understanding Resonance

Your ALB **resonates** when the way you present yourself aligns with who you are and how you show up — consistently, across all the subtle and not-so-subtle touchpoints in your life.

It's not about saying the right thing. It's about being **congruent**. In every setting. With every audience. Even when you think nobody's watching.

And here's the kicker: **resonance isn't determined by you. It's felt by others.**

It's the gut feeling people have after interacting with you — whether through a podcast, a post, or a passing moment in the café queue. Are they drawn to you? Do they trust you? Did they feel you meant what you said? Did your behaviour line up with your values?

That's resonance. And it's more powerful than any slogan or logo could ever be.

Section 2: When Resonance Wobbles

Just like a piano that falls out of tune, resonance can be dulled by even the smallest misalignment. That tiny disconnect between who you say you are and how you act — especially when you think you're off-stage — can erode trust faster than you'd believe.

In an age where authenticity is currency, we're scanning for it more than ever. Our filters are sharp. We're not just craving real — we're *searching* for it. And when we sense a mismatch between your words and your actions, our spidey-sense goes off.

That's not resonance. That's **resistance**.

So in this chapter, we're going to take a close look at your current resonance.

We'll explore:
- What you're projecting (intentionally and unintentionally)
- Where the gaps might lie
- How to bring more congruence between who you are, what you stand for, and how others experience you
- And how small personal incongruences — even on private channels — can quietly erode the trust you've built in your business brand

Because while your personal brand and your business brand are not the same thing, one absolutely can undermine the other. And resonance is the first place you'll feel the tremor.

Section 3: Spotting the Cracks — The Barefoot Influencer

Let me tell you about a case that illustrates this perfectly.

Imagine a high-end fashion footwear brand — glamorous, aspirational, and positioned around confidence, poise, and elegance. They engage an influencer named Chastity to promote their latest range of heels.

Chastity has strong reach, undeniable charisma, and a well-established following. Their account is lively, funny, and candid — but curated.

But one Saturday morning, a tagged Instagram story appears — not on the Chastity's feed, but on her friend's public account. The image? Chastity carrying her stilettos barefoot after a big night out, eyeliner smudged, clearly in recovery mode.

Is she on-brand?

Maybe.

For the right campaign, that image might actually work. It could say: "These heels are so gorgeous I wore them until I couldn't." Or, "These stilettos are so precious I carry them home." There's playfulness, even potential new campaign lines for the shoe brand.

But what if *Chastity's brand* isn't built around the messy realness? What if the audience she's cultivated — or the client who paid her — is expecting sophistication, composure, and aspirational polish?

Now the photo is a **leak**. An uncurated fracture in the brand experience.

The kicker? **The influencer didn't even post it. Their friend did.** This is the Truman Show reality we live in now. You don't control every camera. You don't control every moment that gets shared. But you *can* control your frequency — the consistent signal you broadcast that holds true whether the camera's on you or not.

Section 4: Brand Capital in Action — The Consultancy That Lost the Deal

When private behaviour quietly undermines public opportunity.

A boutique consultancy was in the final running for a seven-figure contract. The pitch was polished. The proposal was flawless. The client loved their ideas.

But someone on the decision-making panel ran a routine social media check of the leadership team. It wasn't a deep dive — just a surface-level scan. And that was all it took.

One of the founders — who was listed as project lead — had a public persona that clashed with the organisation's values. His posts were politically charged. His tone leaned sarcastic. Sprinkled throughout his feed were memes that skirted the edge of culturally inappropriate.

He wasn't cancelled. He hadn't posted anything overtly offensive. But something felt… *off*. Incongruent.

The contract was awarded to another firm.

The feedback?

"Something about the other team felt more aligned."

That's brand capital. It accumulates through consistency and resonance. It erodes through misalignment — even subtly.

It's not always about an obvious mistake or an online "gotcha." Sometimes it's just the unsettling sense that the person you met in the pitch room is not the same person showing up online. When alignment wavers, so does trust. And where trust wavers, opportunity disappears.

Section 5: The Fitness Entrepreneur's Breakdown — And Rebuild

Amy is a client of mine — a solopreneur in the personal fitness space. We've spent years cultivating her brand at the atomic level. Her message is strong, her energy magnetic, and her resonance clear: **resilience, empowerment, and rising stronger**

But during a messy relationship breakdown — her personal life became a target for manipulation. Behind the scenes, she endured gaslighting, harassment, and a slow campaign of social sabotage. Whispers. Phone calls. Cryptic online posts. All of it designed to erode her self-worth and make her question her power.

At first, it worked.

She lashed back. Her posts became defensive. Over-sharing crept in. Her tone online — once uplifting and grounded — grew reactive. Emotional. Erratic.

Then came the messages from clients:

"Are you okay?"

"This doesn't feel like you."

"You've lost your mojo…"

Some clients stopped turning up altogether. The leadership they'd trusted no longer felt safe. The resonance had wobbled.

Fortunately, she caught herself. She recognised the leak — not in her truth, but in *how she was expressing it*. She began rebuilding at the atomic level, grounding herself in the version of her that had always drawn people in: **fierce, focused, and emotionally honest without being emotionally exposed**.

Amy didn't hide her pain — but she curated how it showed up. Her content shifted from venting to victory. From breakdown to rebuilding. Her vulnerability remained, but it was now framed through strength.

And her audience returned. Not just the old clients, but new ones too — drawn to the raw power of a woman who could take a hit, own her story, and stay standing.

The lesson?
Resonance doesn't mean perfection. It means **alignment**. And when your brand has congruence at its core, even your hardest chapters can build loyalty — if you let them reflect your truth with care.

Section 6: Shadow, Signal & Sound — Tuning Your Traits with Intention

Every three-dimensional object casts a shadow. Without it, there's no form — only flatness. Your personal brand is the same. It isn't about polishing yourself into a flawless figure; it's about recognising your full shape, light and dark, and choosing what to amplify.

For example, I have a deeply irreverent sense of humour. It's clever, fast, sometimes inappropriate — and often dark. I find myself chuckling at memes that would make most people uncomfortable. But here's the thing: **I own that part of me. I just don't broadcast it**.

It's not about being fake — it's about being **curated**.

Swearing is another trait I own, but once held back. I used to think I couldn't swear if I wanted to be taken seriously. But in truth, when I swear, it's deliberate. It's punctuation. It's artful. It's authentic to the way I tell stories. And in the right context, it's not only acceptable — it's magnetic. This is one of my once "hidden" traits I choose to amplify, when others wouldn't.

That's the nuance.

There are aspects of myself — like my delight in a wicked joke — that don't fit with my role as an advocate for inclusivity and respect. And yet, I don't disown that side of me. I just choose when and how to share it.

Think of it like the sound engineer at the mixing desk that we talked about earlier: **sliding some channels up, bringing others down**. Not deleting the track but tuning the mix.

Atomic-level branding doesn't require you to amputate parts of yourself. It asks you to be the sound technician of your soul — carefully adjusting your signal so that what comes through is resonant, intentional, and undeniably you.

Section 7: The Demands of Living in the Truman Show

This is the new frontier. Personal brand is no longer what you say about yourself — it's what every connected point of your presence says about you, online and off, **whether you are the person who posted it or not**.

This is especially true for influencers, leaders, and professionals with public personas. Your brand doesn't clock off when you leave the office. When you're the product, the packaging has to be real — and recognisable — 24/7.

Being "on brand" isn't about being fake. It's about **curating your truth so your resonance can consistently deliver value**.

Social platforms often serve us content based on the interests of our friends and followers. So when you engage with problematic content — even passively — it can inadvertently reflect on you.

Don't panic. This isn't about perfection. It's about **awareness**. The goal isn't to hide your shadow — it's to ensure that your visible traits are congruent with your mission, values, and message.

Section 8: Navigating Public Pushback with Congruence

The fitness entrepreneur's story also highlights another hard truth: **when your resonance gets strong, it also gets louder**. The more clearly you stand in your brand, the more visible you become — and that can attract friction.

Gaslighting. Online bullying. Trolling.

These are inevitable for anyone gaining traction in the online space. But when you've done the work of atomic-level branding, you've built more than visibility — you've built a **resonance that rings out like a singing bowl**. It makes flung mud sound off-key.

Your brand becomes your shield.

And even better — it becomes your compass.

When you know your traits, values, and core self, you know exactly how to respond in these moments. You don't over-react. You don't collapse. You hold steady. You decide if the interaction is worth your energy, and if it is, you lean in and answer from alignment.'

Closing Reflection: Congruence is the Goal

Here's what I want you to take away from this chapter:

Your brand resonates when there's alignment between who you are internally and how you show up externally. When those two frequencies match, trust builds. Connection deepens. Opportunities flow.

But when there's even a small mismatch — a moment of incongruence, a leaked behaviour, a pattern that contradicts your promises — resonance wobbles. And people *feel* it, even if they can't articulate why.

The work of aligning your resonance with reality isn't about perfection. It's about **awareness, intention, and consistency**.

It's about recognising that in the Truman Show era, there's no "off stage." Every interaction matters. Every post, every like, every unguarded moment contributes to the frequency you're broadcasting.

So tune carefully. Curate thoughtfully. And most importantly, stay congruent — because that's where the magic happens.

In the next chapter, we'll explore how to live your brand effortlessly, so it stops feeling like work and starts feeling like freedom.

CHAPTER 5 EXERCISES

Exercise 1: Resonance Check — Where Am I Aligned?

Answer these questions honestly:
a. **In which areas of my life does my brand feel most congruent?** (Where do I show up as my truest self?)
b. **Where do I feel like I'm performing or "holding a version" of myself together?**
c. **Are there behaviours or patterns I display when I think no one important is watching that might contradict my brand promise?**
d. **What's one small adjustment I could make this week to bring my behaviour into greater alignment?**

Exercise 2: The Micro-Misalignment Spot Check

Think about your recent online and offline behaviour:
a. **Is there a post I liked or shared recently that felt funny at the time but might be off-brand?**
b. **Have I had any conversations where I performed rather than showed up authentically?**
c. **Is there an "off" comment I made, or a silence that spoke louder than I intended?**
d. **What do these moments tell me about where my resonance might be leaking?**

Exercise 3: The Invisible Audience

Consider the people who see you that you might forget about:
a. **Who sees me that I don't always consider?** (Colleagues, future clients, children, quiet followers on social media, people in the background of my life)
b. **What impression am I leaving on these "invisible" observers?**
c. **If they were asked to describe my brand, what would they say?**
d. **Is that description aligned with how I *want* to be perceived?**

Exercise 4: Shadow Trait Audit

Reflect on the parts of yourself you keep private:
a. **What's one trait I love about myself that I've been unsure how to share publicly?**
b. **How could I express it in a way that strengthens my brand resonance rather than compromising it?**
c. **Are there "shadow" traits — quirks, habits, opinions — I keep private for good reason?** What makes them feel unsharable, and am I making that choice consciously or from fear?
d. **What would it look like to own these traits without broadcasting them inappropriately?**

PART THREE: LIVING ALIGNED

CHAPTER 6:

LIVING IN THE TRUMAN SHOW — WHEN EVERY MOMENT BROADCASTS

Before the internet, before mobile phones, before even colour television — life was lived offline, reputations were built face-to-face, circles of influence were tiny, and personal brands were subtle, if not entirely invisible.

I come from those days. A time when authenticity wasn't a buzzword; it was just... life.

Then social media swept in.

Section 1: Woodstock Online — The Early Days

At first, it felt like **Woodstock online** — peace, love, and random status updates about breathing, farting, headaches, and other inane subjects. No ads. No influencers. Just friends marvelling at the digital echo chamber we'd stumbled into.

We were all toddlers in the new digital playground, gleefully smashing buttons and figuring it out as we went. And we made mistakes. *All of us.*

I trod on digital rakes regularly — sharing a post that didn't land, hitting "like" on something that in hindsight was off-brand (though that language didn't even exist yet), and wondering why I felt so exposed. Every misstep echoed. Not loudly, but enough to give me a creeping sense of being misaligned.

Social media provided a mirror with playback.

That playback inevitably encouraged "tweaks", re-do's... "CTRL-Z".

And before long, what was reflected back at me was a carefully costumed version of myself. I wasn't being dishonest, but I wasn't being *me* either. I was method-acting my way through early online entrepreneurship, wearing a persona that I thought would sell.

Enter Stage Left: IMPOSTER SYNDROME!

It didn't take long before I felt like a fraud. Polished and professional on the outside — but wildly incongruent on the inside. Comparison sickness was contagious through the screen. I wasn't alone in measuring myself against my peers.

Desperation easily creeps in at times like this. Can anyone see me? Hear me? Am I relevant? There's a weird expression of FOMO (Fear Of Missing Out) that can start muddying our authenticity here. It would probably be more appropriately termed *FOBI — Fear Of Being Ignored*. You know it... when you try to join in a chat and get "crickets". When we're misaligned and incongruent, we can fall into the trap of joining the masses. *Beige-ing ourselves!* Joining the hoards to feel part of a tribe. Blending in, and losing ourselves in the process.

To the outside world, this looks "*try-hard*". Trust me... You do *not* want to be a *try-hard*! It feels awful.

The real me — the one with irreverent humour, blunt honesty, and a creatively chaotic brain — was buried under a mask of what I thought the world wanted.

I wasn't in alignment. And it showed.

Section 2: The Shift — When I Found My Frequency

What I've come to realise over the past decade or more of observation is this: **when your personal brand is truly integrated — when it reflects who you are at your core — you no longer need to "act" in order to stay on brand**, regardless of how many brands you may have in the business world.

You're not mentally switching gears between home and work, online and offline, public and private. The tone of your emails matches the tone of your voice. Your LinkedIn bio feels like your actual personality. The brand becomes seamless because it's an extension of you — not a costume.

When you live at atomic-level brand congruence, there's no script required. You're not performing. You're expressing.

This is the heart of effortless personal branding. It's not about being the same person in every room — but about **resonating** in every room. A magnetic, consistent, trusted presence — no matter what the platform or context.

And the ripple effects are extraordinary.

Today, I don't second-guess my posts or agonise over how I'll come across in a pitch meeting. My brand simply *is*. I can feel when I'm in alignment. Conversations are easier. Relationships are richer. Clients find me for the right reasons — and stay because the connection is real.

There's no need to remember who I'm supposed to be. I just show up.

In a world that constantly asks us to shapeshift — to polish, filter, embellish — **living your brand without effort is a radical kind of relief**.

Section 3: Seamless in Every Room

Once your brand is internalised at the atomic level, life becomes refreshingly simple.

You no longer need to consciously "put on" your professional persona. There's no toggling between the polite version of you at work, the cool version of you online, and the real you behind closed doors. You're just... you. In every room.

That doesn't mean you behave identically in every space. It just means you're **congruent**. You don't need to project different versions of yourself to suit the moment — because all the versions stem from the same source.

Same soul, different settings. Same melody, just played at varying volumes. Sometimes fully sound-mixed, sometimes uplugged.

And that brings a kind of liberty you don't know you've been missing until you feel it.

Section 4: Troll by Night — The Cost of Incongruence

Let's take a moment to contrast this ease with the energy drain of incongruence.

We all know someone who plays two parts. By day, a polished professional in client meetings. By night, they're online, lobbing passive-aggressive comments, baiting arguments, or engaging in unkind humour.

They might have convinced themselves it's harmless, cathartic even — "this is my personal profile, after all."

But personal doesn't mean private. Not anymore. The audience is shared.

Even if clients or colleagues never stumble across the comments directly, **incongruence has a scent**. It carries. It shows up in micro-moments: impatience, contradiction, a lingering question in someone's mind that just won't settle.

Incongruence is jarring. And when people sense a mismatch between who you say you are and who you show up as — online, offline, in line at the café — it leaves a kind of festering wound on your brand.

At atomic level, **congruence is the balm**.

It simplifies everything. No more switching masks, second-guessing tone, or editing yourself into submission. You get to laugh loudly, speak clearly, and move freely — because you've done the work to know who you are and how you want to show up.

Section 5: The Ripple Effect — When Congruence Becomes Contagious

When you're clear on your atomic frequency, it reaches further than you think. Your clarity affects the way your colleagues feel about working with you, how your team aligns behind your decisions, how your clients perceive your reliability, and even how your friends trust your advice.

Because people can feel when someone is at ease in their own skin. They feel safe. They lean in.

And as you ripple outward, those around you can feel it's safe to be real too. You model congruence — and give others permission to explore their own.

Section 6: Two-Handed Nuance — Curation vs. Censorship

Of course, congruence doesn't mean full exposure. This isn't about blurting every thought or swearing in a boardroom just because it's "authentic." It's about **nuance**.

There's a kind of wisdom in knowing how to hold the dials of your brand — like a sound engineer with both hands on the desk.

I've talked about my own irreverent humour — how some jokes are, truthfully, hilarious to me, but they stay right where they land: inside. Not because I'm ashamed of my humour, but because some parts of me aren't cohesive with the facets I choose to present. It's a kind of curation. One that honours all of me, while respecting the harmony of the whole.

The same is true of my swearing. I've learned to use it as punctuation — an exclamation mark for storytelling or emphasis. Once upon a time, I held it in, fearing judgement. Now, I know it's part of my voice. I use it with care, not constraint.

This level of self-governance doesn't feel like effort. It feels like intelligence.

Yes, there's an energy cost to self-awareness, but it's not the same as the exhausting effort of wearing a mask (or many). This kind of curation becomes second nature over time. It becomes **integrity in motion**.

The Evolution of Authentic Expression

FROM PERFORMING TO PRESENCE

There's a progression that happens when you do this work deeply:

Stage 1: Performance

You're consciously crafting your brand. You're thinking about every post, every interaction, every word. It feels effortful because it is. You're learning the mechanics of tuning your frequency. But it doesn't feel "hard", because it's natural.

Stage 2: Integration

The conscious effort starts to fade with the old performative habits. Your brand becomes more automatic, more intuitive. You're not constantly second-guessing — you've internalised the framework. You can feel when something's off without having to analyse why.

Stage 3: Presence

You stop "doing" you. You simply *are* you. Your frequency broadcasts naturally, effortlessly. There's no gap between who you are and how you show up. This is alignment.

Most people never reach Stage 3 because they skip Stage 1. They assume authenticity means "just be yourself" without doing the hard work of understanding what "yourself" actually means.

They believe their own press.

But you can't express what you haven't examined. You can't broadcast clearly if you haven't tuned the signal.

Atomic-level branding is the path from performance to presence.

Closing Reflection: Brand, Unblurred

So what does it actually look like to live your brand without effort?

It means waking up each day and not having to remember which version of you the world expects. It means showing up to work, dinner with friends, or a casual scroll online, and knowing that you are recognisably *you* in all those places.

No costume changes. No editing. Just resonance.

Of course, context still matters. The version of me that writes professionally may tighten a turn of phrase or temper an f-bomb. The version that texts my sister is far less filtered. But the resonance remains the same. That's the goal.

When you refine your brand down to its atomic truth, alignment becomes intuitive. Like a tuning fork, you know immediately when something is "off." A brand partnership that doesn't sit right. A caption that feels a little too curated. A networking opportunity that just doesn't hum with harmony.

Living your ALB without effort doesn't mean you never question yourself. It means you **notice faster** when you've veered off course — and gently return.

CHAPTER 6 EXERCISES

Exercise 1: Brand Energy Audit

Let's run a quick systems check.
a. **Where do I feel most in alignment?** (When writing? In client meetings? Late-night phone calls with trusted friends?)
b. **Where do I feel I'm acting or holding a version of myself together?** (Notice the signs — tension in shoulders, rehearsed phrasing, an instinct to "be liked", a fear of being "exposed".)
c. **What parts of my brand feel like "performance," and which feel like "expression"?**
d. **What's one area where I could ease the load by bringing my brand into greater alignment?**

Exercise 2: The Congruence Snapshot

Imagine someone "Googles" you and/or speaks to five people who know you in different contexts. What do they discover?
   a.   **What themes or traits would be mentioned most?**
   b.   **What might surprise them — or contradict their expectations?**
   c.   **Does your digital footprint reinforce my resonance — or dilute it?**

Exercise 3: Living Brand Statement

Write 1–2 sentences that sum up your brand in motion. Not a mission statement, but a vibe.

Example:

"I'm the person who brings sharp insight and warm wit into every room I enter. I lead with empathy, and I don't mask — what you see is what you get, just a little polished."

PART THREE: LIVING ALIGNED

CHAPTER 7:

LETTING YOUR BRAND SPEAK FOR YOU

There's a moment in personal brand development where the gears start to shift.

You stop forcing things.

You stop "putting on your best self."

You stop polishing and pushing and posting from a place of pressure.

And instead, you just *are*.

Your brand doesn't need to be shoved down people's throats. It doesn't need fireworks or flair. It simply needs to **resonate** — deeply, consistently, clearly.

If it doesn't, it's likely a sign that curation is required.

This is the sweet spot of atomic-level branding: when you've done the deep work of uncovering your essence, refined the facets that matter, and committed to showing up as the most aligned version of yourself. From this place, **your brand begins to speak on your behalf**.

Section 1: Trust Earned in Quiet Moments

We often think brand trust is built in big moments — pitches, launches, decisions — but in truth, that's where *attention* is earned. **Trust is more molecular. It's built in the quiet spaces, using reliable cornerstones. It's at the atomic level.**

When your personal brand is congruent, it builds familiarity. Predictability. Safety. Reliability.

And in all branding — as in relationships — **reliability is gold**.

When it's incongruent — even slightly — you'll still have plenty of friends, but those who have a foot in your business camp as well as your friendship circle... well, that mismatch will make them feel a little uneasy.

That's the thing about resonance: when it's absent, there's no frequency left behind. No harmonics humming after you've left the room. No echo.

And if you have overt incongruence, then what's left is static at best — at worst, **fingernails down a blackboard**.

When you are congruent and aligned, you don't need to try to be memorable.

You don't need to be "on."

You just feel complete joy and comfort being who you are.

Section 2: When Resonance Breaks — and Rebuilds

The fitness entrepreneur story from Chapter 5 bears repeating here, because it illustrates something critical: **resonance doesn't mean perfection. It means alignment.**

Her brand was built on resilience and empowerment. But when personal trauma began to bleed into her public expression in ways that felt reactive rather than grounded, her resonance wobbled. Clients sensed it. Some left.

But when she caught herself — when she recognised the leak and began rebuilding from her atomic core — her audience returned. Not just the old clients, but new ones too, drawn to the raw power of a woman who could take a hit, own her story, and stay standing.

The lesson?

When your brand has congruence at its core, even your hardest chapters can build loyalty — if you let them reflect your truth with care.

Section 3: Navigating Public Pushback with Congruence

This story also highlights another hard truth: **when your resonance gets strong, it also gets louder**. The more clearly you stand in your brand, the more visible you become — and that can attract friction.

Gaslighting. Online bullying. Trolling.

These are inevitable for anyone gaining traction in the online space. But when you've done the work of atomic-level branding, you've built more than visibility — you've built a **resonance that rings out like a swami's singing bowl**. It makes flung mud sound off-key.

Your brand becomes your shield.

And even better — it becomes your compass.

When you know your traits, values, and core self, you know exactly how to respond in these moments. You don't over-react. You don't collapse. You hold steady. You decide if the interaction is worth your energy, and if it is, you lean in and answer from alignment.

When Your Brand Becomes Your Compass

THE DECISION-MAKING FILTER

Once your brand is clearly defined at the atomic level, something remarkable happens: **decision-making becomes dramatically easier**.

Not because all decisions are easy. But because you have a clear filter:

Does this opportunity align with my frequency?

Does this partnership resonate with my values?

Does this project amplify traits I want to express, or force me to suppress them?

When the answer is yes, the decision is simple. When it's no, walking away becomes easier.

I can't tell you how many times my ALB has saved me from bad decisions. Partnerships that looked lucrative but felt incongruent. Projects that would have paid well but required me to dim traits I'd worked hard to amplify. Opportunities that were "good" but not "right."

Your brand isn't just how you show up in the world. It's your navigation system.

PART THREE: LIVING ALIGNED

Closing Reflection: Your Brand Is Already Speaking

Here's what I want you to take away from this chapter:

Your brand is already at work. Right now. In this moment.

Every pattern you've established, every promise you've made (spoken or unspoken), every trait you've amplified — it's all broadcasting a frequency that others are tuning into.

The question is: **are you managing that frequency intentionally, or is it managing you?**

When you've done the deep work of atomic-level branding, your brand doesn't need to be announced. It doesn't need to be performed. It simply *is*.

And people feel it.

They trust it.

They remember it.

That's when your brand truly begins to speak for you.

CHAPTER 7 EXERCISES

Exercise 1: Reflection — When Your Brand Speaks

Answer these questions in your journal:
a. **In which spaces (online, offline, work, social settings) does my brand feel most self-sustaining?**
b. **Where do I find myself reverting to effortful "performance"?**
c. **Are there people whose presence triggers me to act out of alignment? Why might that be?**
d. **Am I beginning to see an atomic-level brand scaffold forming?** (An instinctive framework for how to respond, even in hard moments, to remain congruent?)

CHAPTER 8:

STANDING OUT BY STANDING IN

We often assume the key to standing out lies in *more*: more polish, more followers, more charisma, more content. But in reality, the strongest personal brands aren't manufactured — they're **remembered because they're recognised**.

When someone shows up with clarity, consistency, and courageous truth, we *feel* it. It lands. It lingers. And when we talk about brand magnetism, that's what we mean.

Not volume. Not virality.

Resonance.

Section 1: Embracing Your Edges

Remember the day I embraced my PTSD, stood in it, and spoke about it? My psyche still replays the unmistakeable sound of my shattering crystal muumuu, albeit imagined. PTSD is brilliant like that... instant visceral recall.

From that position of frank vulnerability, others suddenly saw my deep empathy and wisdom for what it was, rather than the performative "listen to me" *FOBI* preacher who hid behind her glinting muumuu. My vulnerability was like a font of resonance and relatability that lent clarity to all my stories.

When I stopped trying to insist I was strong and wise — when I dropped the bullshit and said, "here, judge for yourself" — my stories started to land.

This is the power of standing in your truth.

When you no longer need to announce your worth or perform your polish, the signal gets clearer. Magnetism builds not from creating a brand persona, but from chipping away everything that's not true.

Section 2: Authenticity Is a Differentiator

Your quirks are not liabilities. They are **landmarks**. Yet so many people edit out the very traits that would make them memorable — because they don't see those traits reflected in the industry or the influencers around them.

But that's exactly why they matter.

In a world obsessed with filters and sameness, **being honest about who you are (and what you've lived) becomes a radical act**. One that not only differentiates you but makes you trusted.

Magnetism doesn't come from adding — it comes from unmasking.

Not because people love mess, but because **people trust real**.

Section 3: Why "Real" Wins Now More Than Ever

We're living in a strange era where truth and fiction often wear the same coat. Artificial intelligence can write poetry, craft convincing personal bios, and even generate photo-perfect profile pics that never wrinkle, sweat, or blink.

The rise of AI, the misuse of deepfakes, and even the innocent polish of synthetically enhanced selfies have shifted the cultural climate. People are starting to squint at everything. **"Is this real?" is a perpetual online quiz show.**

Authenticity has become magnetic because it's become rare.

We're all becoming expert "truth spotters" without even knowing it — scanning for micro-signs of congruence, instinctively wary of anything that feels too perfect. And when we encounter something that feels unfiltered, unpolished, human? **It stands out like a hand-written letter in a pile of junk mail… and it's just as exciting!**

That's the difference between ALB and persona.

One builds trust. The other begs suspicion.

So, while tech can mimic the movements, cadence, and vocabulary of a human brand, it can't simulate what makes you unforgettable: your weirdness, your edge, your messy grace, your stories lived.

This is why bold authenticity isn't just a nice-to-have — it's the new proof of life.

Section 4: Bold Doesn't Mean Loud

Boldness doesn't always look like confidence or confrontation. Sometimes, it's quiet. Sometimes, it's uncomfortable. **Boldness is having the courage to bring your individuality to the table.**

To allow parts of yourself into the frame that previously lived backstage. To share something that might be misread — but which is true, and important, and yours to tell.

This doesn't mean oversharing. Or turning your brand into a therapy diary. It means choosing, with wisdom, to **stop performing and start expressing**.

Because magnetism comes when people feel like they're getting the real you — unapologetically.

Section 5: The Psychology of Brand Magnetism

Research suggests that psychological magnetism — the quality that draws others in — is built on **perceived authenticity, coherence, and emotional resonance**.

When we see someone behaving congruently with their values, especially under pressure, we instinctively trust them. That trust breeds attraction — not in the superficial sense, but in the **affinity** sense.

People feel safer, more seen, more drawn to those who don't flinch when being themselves.

PART THREE: LIVING ALIGNED

Closing Reflection: Owning the Traits That Truly Differentiate

This chapter has explored the magnetic power of showing up truthfully. But magnetism isn't always obvious. Sometimes, it lives in the parts of you you've learned to downplay.

Take a moment to reflect:

a. **Which of my traits or stories are the most magnetic — where people lean in or open up?**
b. **Have I ever toned something down that later became a surprising source of connection?**
c. **What do I sound like when I stop trying to impress and simply express?**
d. **Are there expressions I once masked that I'm now ready to amplify — because I now understand them as a differentiator?**
e. **And if magnetism is a ripple, which part of my truth is strong enough to start the wave?**

CHAPTER 8 EXERCISES

Exercise 1: The Unmasking Inventory

List three traits, stories, or quirks you've downplayed or hidden because you thought they weren't "professional" or "acceptable."

For each one, ask:
a. **Why did I hide this?**
b. **What would it look like to express this authentically?**
c. **Could this trait actually be a differentiator if I owned it?**

Exercise 2: The Proof of Life Test

In an age of AI and filters, what makes YOU undeniably human and real?
a. **What's a story only I can tell?**
b. **What's a perspective or insight that comes from my lived experience?**
c. **What quirk or edge do I have that can't be replicated?**

Exercise 3: Magnetism Audit

Reflect on moments when you've felt most magnetic — when people were drawn to you effortlessly:
a. **What was I doing?**
b. **What traits was I expressing?**
c. **How can I bring more of that energy into my brand consistently?**

PART THREE: LIVING ALIGNED

CHAPTER 9:

THE HONESTY IMPERATIVE — TUNING IN PRIVATE

Here's something I need you to understand deeply, fundamentally, at the cellular level:

The work of atomic-level branding requires brutal honesty. And you are under no obligation to share this work with anyone else.

This is your private tuning process. Your workshop. Your laboratory. The place where you can admit things you'd never say out loud. Where you can acknowledge traits you've been taught to be ashamed of. Where you can explore the fullness of who you are — shadow and light — without fear of judgement.

If being confrontational, for example, is a happy hobby for you, then own that here. No-one else needs to read this.

If there's a part of your humour that's dark or inappropriate, acknowledge it here. If you're angrier than you'd like to be, more insecure, more jealous, more ambitious, more selfish — **write it down**.

Because you can't tune what you won't acknowledge.

Section 1: Why Privacy Matters for This Work

When we know others will see our work, we edit. We censor. We perform — even in our private journals, if we think someone might stumble across them someday.

But atomic-level branding demands **raw, unfiltered honesty**. It requires you to look at the parts of yourself you've been taught to hide and decide — consciously, strategically — which ones to amplify, which ones to manage, and which ones to keep private.

You can't do that work if you're worried about being judged.

So let me give you permission right now: **this work is for you alone**. No one else needs to see your trait sorting document. No one else needs to know which parts of yourself you're wrestling with. No one else needs access to your internal tuning process.

This is the space where you get to be completely, painfully, liberatingly honest.

Section 2: The Permission To Be Messy

One of the most damaging myths about personal branding is that you need to have it all figured out before you begin.

That's bullshit.

Atomic-level branding isn't about perfection. It's about **clarity**. And clarity comes from sitting with the mess, not avoiding it.

So give yourself permission to:
- Discover traits you don't like about yourself
- Acknowledge behaviours you're not proud of
- Admit fears, insecurities, and contradictions
- Explore the full spectrum of who you are without needing to justify it

This isn't about wallowing. It's about **seeing clearly** so you can tune accurately.

Section 3: The Things We Hide — And Why They Matter

Let me share some of the things I've had to acknowledge in my own tuning process:

I suffer blind fury. It's not a trait I love, but it's there. And by acknowledging it, I've built systems to manage it so it doesn't sabotage my brand.

I have an irreverent sense of humour. Some of the things I find hilarious would horrify others. I don't broadcast this publicly, but I don't deny it privately either. It's part of my frequency.

I can be blunt to the point of harshness. I've learned to soften my delivery, but the instinct is still there. Acknowledging it helps me choose when to lean into it (in contexts where directness is valued) and when to dial it back.

I carried undiagnosed PTSD for years. Naming it, standing in it, and speaking about it openly transformed my brand. It gave context to my empathy and depth to my insights.

None of these are things I'm "supposed" to say in a business book. But they're true. And by acknowledging them privately first, I gained the power to decide how — and whether — to express them publicly.

Section 4: The Brutal Honesty Audit

Here's an exercise I want you to do, in private, right now:

Make a list of traits, behaviours, or patterns you've never admitted to anyone.

Things like:
- "I secretly judge people who..."
- "I'm more jealous than I'd like to be about..."
- "I have a habit of..."
- "I'm insecure about..."
- "I sometimes think..."

Don't censor. Don't soften. Don't make excuses.

Just write.

Because until you see these things clearly, you can't decide what to do with them. And some of them — maybe even most of them — aren't liabilities at all. They're just parts of you that haven't been tuned yet.

Section 5: Deciding What to Amplify, Manage, or Keep Private

Once you've done the brutal honesty audit, the next step is **categorisation**.

For each trait or pattern you've identified, ask:

1. Does this serve my goals and align with my values?

If yes, it might be something to amplify — to lean into more publicly.

2. Does this create static or undermine my brand promise?

If yes, it's something to manage — to build systems around so it doesn't sabotage you.

3. Is this something I can own privately without broadcasting it?

If yes, keep it private. Not everything needs to be shared. You can acknowledge a trait without making it part of your public brand.

This isn't about denial. It's about **curation**.

You get to decide which parts of your frequency to broadcast loudly, which to express selectively, and which to keep as background harmonics that only you can hear.

Section 6: The Freedom of Brutal Honesty

Here's the paradox: **the more honest you are with yourself in private, the freer you become in public**.

When you've acknowledged all the messy, complicated, contradictory parts of yourself — when you've sorted them, examined them, and decided how to manage them — you stop being afraid of being "found out."

There's nothing to hide, because you've already seen it all. You've already made peace with it. You've already built systems to manage what needs managing and amplified what deserves amplifying.

That's when your brand becomes effortless.

Atomic-Level Branding is not just about "knowing yourself". It's about "living yourself", at all times — rather than performing a brand promise.

Because you're not performing. You're not hiding. You're just **tuned**. Remember that you are three dimensional. That requires your shadow traits to be held and recognised — even amplified, if that's your thing — for your ALB to be authentic.

Closing Reflection: This Is Your Safe Space

Let me say it one more time, because it's critical:

This work is private. No one else needs to see it. You are safe to be brutally honest here.

If you like swearing, own it here.

If you have dark humour, acknowledge it here.

If you're angrier, more insecure, more ambitious, more flawed than you'd ever admit publicly — **write it down here**.

Because this is where the real tuning happens. This is where you gain clarity. This is where you take control of your frequency instead of letting it control you.

And once you've done this work — once you've seen yourself clearly and decided consciously how to express each facet — you'll find that living your brand becomes not just effortless, but **liberating**.

PART THREE: LIVING ALIGNED

CHAPTER 9 EXERCISES

Exercise 1: The Brutal Honesty Audit

In a private document (one you'll never share), complete these prompts:
   a. **Traits I've never admitted to anyone:**
   b. **Behaviours I'm not proud of:**
   c. **Insecurities I hide:**
   d. **Judgements I secretly hold:**
   e. **Parts of myself I've been taught to be ashamed of:**

Don't censor. Just write.

Exercise 2: Categorising the Hidden

For each item from your audit, decide:
- **Amplify:** Could this actually be a strength if I owned it?
- **Manage:** Do I need systems to keep this from sabotaging me?
- **Keep Private:** Is this something I can own without broadcasting?

Exercise 3: Building Management Systems

Choose one trait you want to manage (like my anger management):
a. **What's the trait?**
b. **When does it create problems?**
c. **What's my early warning sign that it's emerging?**
d. **What system can I build to redirect it?**

....

....

....

....

....

....

....

....

....

CHAPTER 10:

BEHAVIOUR AS BRAND — THE INTEGRITY LOOP

Your behaviour *is* your brand.
Not what you say. Not what you post. Not what you claim to value.
Your behaviour.

The way you treat people when you think no one important is watching. The promises you keep (or break) when it's inconvenient. The consistency between your stated values and your actual choices.

This is where brand congruence either solidifies or shatters.

The Business Impact of Personal Congruence

WHEN PERSONAL BRAND ELEVATES BUSINESS BRAND

Let me share a success story from a Financial Planner I've worked with.

Darryl had always kept his personal and professional lives completely separate. LinkedIn was buttoned-up, conservative, strictly business. His personal Facebook was full of mountain biking photos, craft beer reviews, and goofy dad jokes.

He thought this was smart — protecting his professional credibility by keeping the "fun" stuff private.

But when we dug into his atomic-level brand, we discovered something interesting: his best clients *loved* his sense of adventure and his approachability. Those weren't liabilities — they were differentiators in an industry full of stuffy, impersonal advisors.

So we integrated. Not conflated — integrated. Darryl started sharing stories about financial planning for adventure travel. He posted about teaching his kids about money using craft beer brewing as a metaphor. He let his personality show through without abandoning professionalism.

The result? His business doubled in 18 months.

Because people don't just want a financial advisor. They want a financial advisor they *like*. They want someone who feels human, relatable, trustworthy.

And trustworthy doesn't mean perfect. It means **congruent**.

When his personal authenticity started showing up in his business brand, people relaxed. They trusted him more. They referred him more. They stuck around longer.

That's the power of congruence: it doesn't just protect your brand. It elevates it.

Section 1: The Personal vs. Business Brand Distinction

Let me be clear: **your personal brand and your business brand are not the same thing.**

But they're deeply interconnected.

Your business brand is the promise your company or service makes to customers. Your personal brand is the promise *you* make — as a human, a leader, a presence in the world.

When these two are in **congruence** — when your personal behaviour aligns with your business values — they reinforce each other. Trust compounds. Credibility deepens.

But when they're **incongruent** — when your personal behaviour contradicts your business brand — both suffer.

Section 2: The Danger of Conflation

The trap many people fall into is **conflating** their personal and business brands — believing they're one and the same.

This leads to two problems:

1. You become a slave to your business brand.

You feel like you can never be human, never make mistakes, never express anything that doesn't fit the polished business image. This is exhausting and unsustainable.

2. You assume your personal behaviour doesn't affect your business.

You think you can separate your "work self" from your "real self," posting whatever you want on personal social media or behaving however you want in private. But in the Truman Show era, there's no such thing as separate spheres.

The goal isn't conflation. It's **congruence**.

Your personal and business brands should be aligned — singing in harmony, not unison. They don't have to be identical, but they can't contradict each other.

If anyone needs any further evidence of how swiftly incongruence can ruin a career, simply reflect on the cataclysmic downfalls of modern sports stars who choose influencer roles without working on their ALB: How many big name sports stars can you think of who've ended up "cancelled" or "dropped" due to off-screen indiscretions that jar with "gig" personas?

In contrast, reflect on Aussie cricketing great, David "Boony" Boon... an iconic name who proudly owned drinking 73 beers on the Sydney-Heathrow flight ahead of any Ashes Test. Boony was congruent. And we loved him for it.

Section 3: The Integrity Loop

Here's how congruence creates what I call the **Integrity Loop**:
Your values inform **your behaviour**.
Your behaviour creates **patterns**.
Patterns create **promises** (brand).
Kept promises build **trust**.
Trust creates **opportunity**.
Opportunity reinforces **values**.

This is a virtuous cycle. When each element aligns, the loop strengthens. Your brand becomes self-reinforcing, self-sustaining, and magnetic.

But if any element breaks — if your behaviour doesn't match your values, if your patterns don't keep your promises — the loop fractures. Trust erodes. Opportunities disappear.

Section 4: Examples of Congruent vs. Incongruent Behaviour

Congruent Example:

A business consultant whose brand is built on "clarity and simplification" communicates with clients in clear, jargon-free language. Their emails are concise. Their proposals are easy to understand. Their social media posts explain complex ideas simply. **Behaviour matches brand.**

Incongruent Example:

That same consultant sends confusing, overly technical emails to clients. Their proposals are dense and hard to parse. Their social media posts are filled with industry jargon. **Behaviour contradicts brand.**

Even if the work itself is excellent, the incongruence creates friction. Clients feel uneasy. They start to wonder: "Do you actually value clarity, or is that just marketing?"

Section 5: The Social Media Minefield

Nowhere is the personal/business brand tension more visible than on social media.

Many people believe their "personal" accounts are separate from their "professional" presence. But personal doesn't mean private anymore. **The audiences overlap.**

If your business brand is built on inclusivity, respect, and collaboration — but your personal social media is filled with divisive political rants, mean-spirited jokes, or aggressive arguments — people notice. Even if they don't comment. Even if they don't unfollow.

They feel the incongruence. And it weakens trust.

This doesn't mean you can't have political opinions or a sense of humour. It just means you need to be **intentional** about how you express them, knowing that your personal behaviour reflects on your business brand whether you like it or not.

Section 6: How to Maintain Congruence (Not Conflation)

Here's how to keep your personal and business brands aligned without losing yourself:

1. Identify your non-negotiable values.

What do you stand for, both personally and professionally? Where's the overlap? These are your anchors.

2. Audit your behaviour across all contexts.

Are you treating people with the same respect in private as you do in public? Are your social media habits aligned with your stated values?

3. Create conscious boundaries.

Decide what parts of your personal life you want to keep private. You don't have to share everything — but what you *do* share should be congruent.

4. When in doubt, ask: "Does this behaviour strengthen or weaken my brand promise?"

If it weakens it, reconsider. Not out of fear, but out of integrity.

Closing Reflection: Behaviour Is the Brand

You can have the best logo, the sharpest tagline, the most polished website in the world. But if your behaviour doesn't match your brand promise, none of it matters.

People trust what you do, not what you say.

And in the Truman Show era — where everything is visible, everything is recorded, everything is potentially public — your behaviour *is* your brand.

So ask yourself:

Does my behaviour reflect my values?
Do my patterns keep my promises?
Is my personal brand in congruence with my business brand?

If the answer is yes, you're in the Integrity Loop of ALB. Keep going.

If the answer is no, you know what to do.

Tune.

CHAPTER 10 EXERCISES

Exercise 1: The Integrity Loop Audit

Map your own Integrity Loop:
a. **My core values:**
b. **Behaviours that reflect those values:**
c. **Patterns I've created:**
d. **Promises those patterns make:**
e. **Is trust being built or eroded?**

Exercise 2: Personal vs. Business Brand Alignment

Answer these questions:
a. **What does my business brand promise?**
b. **What does my ALB communicate?**
c. **Where do they align?**
d. **Where might they contradict?**
e. **What's one adjustment I can make to bring them into greater congruence?**

Exercise 3: Social Media Congruence Check

Review your last 20 social media posts (personal and professional):
a. **Do they reflect my stated values?**
b. **Is there anything I've posted or engaged with that might create friction with my business brand?**
c. **What's one habit I could shift to ensure greater congruence?**

CHAPTER 11:

EVOLUTION WITHOUT LOSS — STAYING TRUE WHILE GROWING

Your brand — your true, atomic-level brand — isn't something you build once and forget about.
It's alive. It grows as you do.
It moves with the seasons of your life and business. And like any organic force, if left untended for too long, it can become overgrown, outdated, or simply misaligned.

But that doesn't mean you need to throw it out and start over.

Section 1: The Diamond Doesn't Change — The Setting Does

A diamond forged under pressure may look, at a glance, like a piece of cut glass. But it is thousands of times more resilient. It won't erode. It can't be scratched. It will outlast nearly everything it encounters.

Your core truth is your diamond.

Never forget that.

The setting may change. The way you present your diamond to the world might shift as you grow, as your audience evolves, as your goals change.

But the stone? **The stone remains.**

Section 2: Growth Doesn't Mean Abandonment

Too many people believe that evolving their brand means abandoning who they were. That growth requires erasure. That if you want to level up, you have to leave your old self behind.

That's not growth. That's **reinvention**. And reinvention requires performance, and performance breaks trust.

Your audience — whether it's one person or one million — fell in love with your frequency. They tuned into your signal because something about it resonated with them.

When you evolve *with* your core intact, they'll evolve with you. They'll trust that even though you're growing, you're still *you*.

But when you abandon your core — when you try to become someone else entirely — they feel the disconnection. The resonance breaks. And they'll leave, not because you changed, but because you became unrecognisable.

Section 3: How to Evolve Without Losing Your Frequency

Here's the key: **Evolution is about tuning, not transformation.**

You're not changing your frequency. You're refining it. You're adjusting the amplitude on certain traits. You're adding new harmonics while keeping the fundamental tone the same.

Ask yourself:

1. What are my non-negotiable core traits?

These are the foundations — the traits that define you no matter what context you're in. Guard these fiercely.

2. What new traits or skills am I developing?

As you grow, you'll acquire new capabilities, perspectives, and strengths. These are additions, not replacements.

3. Are there old patterns I've outgrown?

Some behaviours that served you in the past might not serve you now. Release them with gratitude, not guilt.

4. How can I communicate this evolution to my audience?

You don't need to issue a press release every time you grow. But you do need to stay congruent. Let your evolution show up naturally in your work, your content, your interactions.

Section 4: Checking for Alignment Drift

Evolution is inevitable. But sometimes, without realising it, we drift *away* from our core rather than building *on* it.

Here's how to check for alignment drift:

Revisit your atomic-level brand traits.

The ones you identified in Chapter 4. Do they still feel true? Have any new traits emerged that feel more "me" than what you've been projecting?

Audit your recent behaviour and content.

Does it still reflect your values? Or have you started performing a version of yourself that feels less authentic?

Ask trusted friends or clients:

"Do I still feel like the same person you met [X years ago]? Or have I changed in ways that feel incongruent?"

If you've drifted, don't panic. Just tune back.

Section 5: The Permission to Evolve

Let me give you explicit permission: **You are allowed to grow.**

You're allowed to change your mind.

You're allowed to learn new things that shift your perspective.

You're allowed to outgrow old beliefs, old patterns, old versions of yourself.

But do it consciously. Do it with integrity. And do it in a way that honours the core frequency you were born with.

Because change that abandons your core isn't evolution — it's fragmentation and mimicry.

But growth that deepens your core? That's **alignment**.

Closing Reflection: The Living Brand

Your ALB isn't a monument. It's a living, breathing frequency that evolves as you do.

The work isn't to freeze yourself in amber, desperately clinging to who you were five years ago. The work is to stay tuned — constantly listening to your own signal, adjusting as needed, and ensuring that as you grow, your core remains intact.

You were born with everything you need.

The clarity, the value, the resonance — all of it is inherent, waiting to be curated.

This journey hasn't been about adding layers, but about cutting through the noise, chiseling off performative habits. Polishing what is already within. Letting it shine, without apology.

You aren't creating a brand. **You are one. You always were.**

Now, you own it — at the atomic level.

CHAPTER 11 EXERCISES

Exercise 1: Core vs. Context Audit

Answer these questions:
a. **What are my non-negotiable core traits?** (The foundations that define me)
b. **What traits or skills have I developed recently?** (New additions)
c. **What patterns have I outgrown?** (What I'm ready to release)
d. **How can I communicate this evolution authentically?**

Exercise 2: Alignment Drift Check

Reflect on where you are now vs. where you were a year ago:
a. **Do my current behaviours still align with my stated values?**
b. **Have I started performing a version of myself that feels less authentic?**
c. **What feedback have I received that suggests drift?**
d. **What's one adjustment I can make to tune back to my core?**

Exercise 3: The Diamond Test

Close your eyes and think about your core truth — the diamond at the centre of your brand.
a. **What is unchangeable about me?**
b. **What setting am I currently presenting this diamond in?**
c. **Does the setting honour the diamond, or obscure it?**
d. **What would it look like to polish the diamond while updating the setting?**

PART THREE: LIVING ALIGNED

EPILOGUE:

ALIGNED AF

You made it.
You've done the work. You've tuned your frequency. You've identified your traits, sorted them, refined them. You've aligned your resonance with reality. You've examined your behaviour, your patterns, your promises.

You've been brutally honest with yourself. You've acknowledged the shadow and the light. You've built systems to manage what needs managing and amplified what deserves amplifying.

And now?

Now you're **Aligned AF**.

What "Aligned AF" Means

Aligned AF isn't about perfection. It's not about having every facet polished to a mirror shine. It's not about never making mistakes or never feeling off-tune.

Aligned AF is the state of being fully aligned with your authentic frequency — living, breathing, and expressing your brand without effort or performance.

When you're Aligned AF:

- Your brand isn't something you *do*; it's who you *are*
- You don't need to remember which version of yourself to be in different contexts
- You trust your instincts because they're tuned to your core
- You attract the right people and repel the wrong ones — and you're okay with that
- You can weather criticism, pushback, and trolls without losing your centre
- You evolve without losing yourself

Aligned AF is freedom.

The Frequency You Were Born With

Your brand isn't about shouting louder than everyone else. It's about tuning into your authentic frequency and transmitting it so clearly, so consistently, that the people who resonate with it can't help but tune in.

You were born with that frequency. It's been with you since your first cry. It's in your quirks, your humour, your way of seeing the world, your deepest values, your messiest contradictions.

And for most of your life, you've been taught to muffle it. To smooth it down. To fit into boxes that were never built for your shape.

This book has been about unlearning that.

About stripping away the static. Removing the interference. Tuning back into the signal you were born to transmit.

The Work Continues

Here's the truth: tuning your frequency isn't a one-time event. It's a practice.

You'll drift. Life will throw you off-centre. New opportunities will tempt you to perform rather than resonate. Old patterns will creep back in.

But now you have the tools to notice. To pause. To tune back.

You have your trait matrix. Your brutal honesty audit. Your integrity loop. Your congruence checklist.

You have the awareness to know when you're aligned and when you're not.

And most importantly, **you have permission** — permission to be messy, to be flawed, to be recognising bum-notes internally while curating thoughtfully in public.

What Happens When You're Aligned AF

When you're truly aligned with your authentic frequency, something magical happens:

Opportunities find you.

Because your signal is so clear, the right people can't help but tune in. You stop chasing and start attracting.

Decisions become easier.

Because you know your core values, you can quickly assess whether an opportunity, partnership, or project aligns with your frequency.

Relationships deepen.

Because you're no longer performing, people feel safe being real with you. Trust builds faster. Connection goes deeper.

Work feels effortless.

Not easy — but effortless. Because you're not constantly code-switching, masking, or trying to be someone you're not. You're just *you*, fully expressed.

Life gets lighter.

Because you've released the weight of trying to be all things to all people. You've accepted that your frequency will attract some and repel others — and that's exactly as it should be.

The Ripple Effect

When you're aligned at an atomic frequency, you create ripples that affect everyone around you.

Your clients feel safer being authentic.

Your colleagues feel permission to drop their masks.

Your children see what it looks like to live congruently.

Your friends experience what true resonance feels like.

You become proof that it's possible to be fully yourself *and* wildly successful.

That authenticity isn't a liability — it's a superpower.

That tuning your frequency isn't selfish — it's the most generous thing you can do. Because when you're aligned, you give others permission to align too.

Final Words: This Is a Homecoming

I want to leave you with this thought:

Atomic-level branding isn't about becoming someone new. It's about coming home to who you've always been.

It's about recognising the frequency you were born with and giving yourself permission to broadcast it clearly, consistently, unapologetically.

It's about chiselling away the beige, the static, the interference — and revealing the brilliant, one-of-a-kind signal that's been there all along.

You weren't born to blend in. You weren't born to broadcast someone else's frequency. You weren't born to muffle your magic.

You were born to be Aligned AF.

And now? Now you know how.

So go. Tune your frequency. Live your brand. Resonate deeply.

The world doesn't need another carefully curated persona.

It needs you. Your voice. Your frequency. Your truth.

Aligned AF.

Want to continue your work?

BOOK YOUR DISCOVERY CALL

ACKNOWLEDGEMENTS

To every person who's ever told me I was "too much' or "not enough' — thank you. You helped me understand the power of reframing.

To every client who trusted me with their atomic-level tuning — thank you. Your courage to be unflinchingly honest with yourself inspired this book.

To my daughter, who taught me that there are infinite ways to express creativity, and no single 'right' path.

To those who supported Steve and me during our darkest period — you know who you are. Your private messages of encouragement, your refusal to engage with the mob, and your quiet confidence in our character gave us the strength to weather the storm. Thank you.

To my father, whose wisdom I didn't fully understand until years later: you were right. I could never be Steve. But more importantly, I needed to learn to be fully, unapologetically myself.

To Steve: for being my rock, my partner, and my constant reminder that authenticity is more powerful than any performance. You never wavered, even when I did.

To anyone who has ever been targeted by cancel culture, gaslighting, or coordinated harassment: this book is for you. You are not alone. Your truth matters. And you deserve to build from a foundation that no troll can shake.

And to you, reader — thank you for doing this work. For being brave enough to look at yourself honestly, to tune your frequency with care, and to show up in the world as who you truly are.

The world does not need any more beige. It needs more *you*.

Stay Aligned.

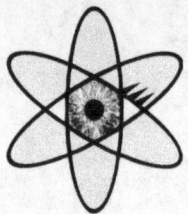

About the Author

Jo Starling is an award-winning creative strategist, designer, and business mentor who has spent three decades helping founders turn raw, lived truth into unmistakable market signal. She works at the intersection of identity, language, and visibility — translating messy human brilliance into offers, brands, and leadership presence that hold under pressure.

Her work has been recognised through multiple business awards spanning entrepreneurialism, creative services, business excellence, and leadership. She built her early career and award-winning business life in Darwin, Northern Territory — a place that shaped her grit, humour, and straight-talking clarity — before relocating in 2012 to the far south coast of New South Wales with her daughter and her husband, Steve.

Outside the studio and coaching room, Jo is an avid angler with a global appetite for "the next big thing" (which is always a fish). That pursuit runs parallel to her work: a relentless devotion to reading conditions, trusting instinct, and refining craft — not to become someone else, but to become more precisely herself.

www.ingramcontent.com/pod-product-compliance
Lightning Source LLC
Chambersburg PA
CBHW011150290426
44109CB00025B/2561